P|

YOU CAN'T M

D1489041

"Denise Messineo has written the book that every HR leader wants to write—a hilarious and head-shaking collection of crazy employee mishaps. Without a doubt, you can't make this sh*t up!"

STEVE ARNESON, Ph.D., President, Arneson Leadership Consulting and author of *Bootstrap Leadership* and *What Your Boss Really Wants From You*

"Filled with stories that are sometimes outrageous, funny, sad, and above all, relatable to human behavior as reflected in recent head-lines, You Can't Make This Sh*t Up *shows the other side of HR beyond benefits, handbooks, and performance reviews! A must-read for anyone in a leadership role or interested in a career in HR or simply looking for a fun read."*

BECKY BLALOCK, Managing Partner of Advisory Capital, board member, former Sr. VP and CIO of Southern Company, and author of the bestselling book *DARE, Straight Talk on Confidence, Courage, and Career for Women in Charge*

"Denise always had the ability to take real life experiences in the workplace and turn them into valuable lessons for our employees and our company. She had the ability to use these true stories, along with her leadership skills, to create and establish a high performance culture that drove our company's success. This book will provide you with a simple common-sense approach to leadership and employee development."

JERE BROWN, CEO Americas (Retired), Dimension Data

YOU CAN'T
MAKE THIS SH*T UP

MASCOT® BOOKS

www.mascotbooks.com

For more information, please contact:
Mascot Books
620 Herndon Parkway #320
Herndon, VA 20170
info@mascotbooks.com

Library of Congress Control Number: 2018900815

CPSIA Code: PBANG0418A
ISBN-13: 978-1-63177-980-0

Printed in the United States

You Can't Can't Make This Sh*t Up

Tales From The HR Crypt

Unearthed By Denise Messineo

This book is dedicated to my family. Tony, for the lifetime
of full support enabling me to reach for the stars and
achieve my life dreams. My friends aptly nicknamed you
St. Anthony. I'll love you forever.

To my daughter and son, Lysa Messineo Gorgen and Brian
Messineo. You loved my stories from work and life and
encouraged me to tell them. I'll never forget our dinner-
time conversations as you grew up!

In recognition of HR Professionals everywhere: you are the
heart and conscience of every organization.

ACKNOWLEDGMENTS

First of all, I thank my husband, Tony; our two children, Lysa and Brian; their spouses, Kevin and Kristin; and our seven beautiful grandchildren, Lily, Geaton, Enzo, Sonny, Marco, Camilla, and Layla, for their unwavering support and patience while I escaped alone to the beach house to write this book. You are all the source of my joy and I cannot imagine getting this accomplished without your encouragement and curiosity of "how's the book coming?" I am blessed with an incredible family and the best sounding board ever in my longest friendship. Linda Stuart, thank you, thank you. I love you all with my entire being.

Next, I must thank my former CEO and COO, Jere Brown and Wes Johnston for constantly giving me fodder for the book and also encouraging me over the years to write it. Both of you are fabulous leaders, coaches, and friends. I am blessed to have had the opportunity to work with you. So many folks have given me stories and support, too many to name. You know who you are and I've thanked you privately. However, one in particular has called and texted me constantly during the past year with story after story: Jeff Kwiatkowski, one of the funniest guys you'll ever meet and a true friend. The last HR team I had the pleasure and honor of working with—we laughed, we stressed, we survived! Thanks for the great memories and the great work you did with me. The work continues...

There is no question that this book would not have been possible without the recommendation from my good friend, Edmund Nnaemeka Okwuchukwu, to contact Naren Aryal with Mascot Books, my publisher. Naren and his entire staff were encouraging, patient, and simply the best group of folks to work with ever! Thanks to you, the stories are unearthed!

THE AUTHOR'S STORY

I have spent many years in leadership roles, some in Operations and some in HR. This book is a compilation of the stories about people and what they do at work instead of what they are being paid to do. These stories come from colleagues, friends, and family after years and years of interviews, conversations, and real-life experience. I often joked about writing a book like this, and now it's here.

My working career started at a dry cleaning company, of all places. I was a full-time "spotter," and myself and my co-worker, a male 25 years my senior, went to "spotting school" together. I later learned he was being paid almost double what I was earning. The reason given was that "he has a wife and three kids to support, while it's just you and your husband." Well, those who know me know it took no time at all for me to find a better place to work.

I found my way to a national insurance carrier and worked my way up to a territorial manager who was responsible for the profit and loss in a three state region. While there, I also obtained my college degree. While I found myself there due to a discriminatory act, it was the best thing that ever happened to me since it got me on the right track to be a strong leader.

After a long tenure, I moved to another insurance carrier. I loved my new role, which was responsible for operations in their legal offices across the country. I eventually moved to another role where I worked myself out of a job and was laid off. While disappointing, everything happens for a reason and I found myself at a progressive IT company thanks to a friend I met while earning my master's degree. That was truly the best thing that ever happened to me. I learned a lot, earned a lot, and met some great people along the way.

Unfortunately, my time there came to an end. While I loved my job and the team I worked with, there were folks at the very top of the organization who I felt struggled to live the values of the company. We parted ways and life moved on.

When I left my most recent role, my colleagues gave me a beautiful book of photos and stories from my time there. I asked permission to include the comments from a former colleague (she left the company many years before me) and she agreed. Here are her comments:

I can't believe it's been 16 years since we first met. This was when XX acquired ZZ in 2001 and we were all thrown together. Lots of crazy things have happened since then. The first thing I recall after we (ZZ) were acquired was that XX marketing put socks on everyone's desk, with a note saying XX will knock your socks off. Clever idea, but the timing was a bit off as we were in the middle of layoffs and were giving people the boot!!! You can only imagine how well those socks were received.

Remember we had the first HR meeting with KA? Oh boy, what a day that was. And another great example of how to treat people—we were all gathered there, in the conference room of the hotel. There were HR people from 5 or 6 different companies, who had never met before, coming together for the very first time to build one great HR team. And then, our fierce leader, KA, put up an org chart that literally not one person in that room had seen before or had had a conversation about. People were put in new jobs, people lost responsibilities, reporting lines changed, it was mayhem. Every single person was upset, including me because she gave me benefits! Really, that was not going to happen! Thankfully, some adjustments were quickly made, including not giving me benefits. And that was just the beginning of our journey with XX.

Late 2002 or early 2003, you replaced DH as head of HR for the US. That cannot have been easy on you, because a lot of people were upset that he had to go (including me—he is great guy and brilliant HR person). And in addition, many other HR people were retrenched. I was pregnant and I can still clearly remember how well you handled that mess. You earned respect by being understanding, patient, and kind. When I was also retrenched (much to my delight), you ensured that the timing of it all would be most beneficial to me so that I could have benefits while I had my baby. I really respected you for how you discussed all the options with me and I felt no stress at all. Not long after my baby was born, you hired me back on a consulting basis and gave me the best of both worlds: the flexibility to take care of my children and ability to do the work I love to do.

Then on a train from DC to NY you asked me to take responsibility for recruitment. You must have read the horri-fied expression on my face, because you quickly added: you don't have to recruit, I know you hate that, I just need you to manage the function. The great thing is that you always just let me do my own thing, gave me the room to do my job, but were always there for guidance and for bouncing off ideas. I can't recall one single time we had a major disagreement. Not even when you had to stage an intervention between myself *and another HR person on the team. That was fun! Thankfully you had a lot of understanding for my Dutch directness.*

You had to rebuild your team a number of times due to all the changes and turmoil. I remember you were interviewing this girl one time, and after the interview you said, "oh, those huge earrings! I don't remember a word of what she was saying because I got so distracted by those earrings!" We shared a good laugh over that one.

You called me one summer while I was visiting Europe to tell me about an international opportunity. This was another example of your professional generosity. You don't hold people back. Rather, you allow them to take the plunge...

Well, it started out very typical of what was to come. Our fierce leader (name intentionally withheld) insisted that I start on December 1st. Arriving with our two kids in an unknown country before Christmas only to find out that everyone goes on summer vacation on December 2nd! Really?! Anyway, we spent the holidays in the sun in an empty house and were the only ones in the office. That was why I was one of the first to find out you had a situation in the US. The CEO decided to walk out in early January and ended up taking half the management team with him to start a new competitive business. Surprisingly, he had no employment contract so there was no recourse for solicitation and competition. And of course, the blame for that our darling HR leader tried to pin on you and legal, but it was quickly diverted since the international HR leader owned the CEO contracts.

Six months into my international assignment, you came to the office and I had a complete meltdown over the failing relationship with my leader there. For me, it was quite the change in work environment. Morale and culture were terrible and toxic and I broke down in tears in the office. I was so happy you were there, because the situation was quite tense. The conversation gave me strength and fighting power for years to come. This made me stronger and able to deal with the situation in a constructive way. I never had a breakdown again (and consequently moved to another role under a different leader). I still have the wish fairy doll that you gave me. She sits on the shelf in my home office with her necklace that says Celebrate You. Every time I look at her, she makes me smile and she reminds me of you.

Remember the global meetings and a leader wearing a black thong under white pants, which was visible every time she bent over. You were horrified! (And so were we all.) I think this was also the meeting the leader chewed out the guest speaker. Remember that? We made the best out of those meetings—they were not fun.

I must say, I don't think there will be many people who have seen it all and have been put in so many challenging situations like you. You have handled it with determination, empathy, grace, and kindness, however tough that was. I really can't wait to read your book...

That is all from a former employee, then colleague, and now dear friend.

Enjoy the stories! I'm sure you'll be reminded of craziness at your work. Sometimes, you just can't make this sh*t up!

Denise

CONTENTS

CRIME &
PUNISHMENT

MURDER, SHE WROTE

It was a sunny October morning. The senior VP of HR was enjoying her second cup of coffee, leisurely reading the Saturday paper. Her cell phone rang and she did not know the number.

The caller was difficult to understand and his voice was cracking. "Hello, Jan? This is Dan. I have some terrible news. Ed died in a house fire last night. I am so upset; we were so close! I'm driving home from Tom's funeral, and then I learn about this. I just don't know what to say or do."

Jan: Dan, I am so, so sorry! I just can't believe it! I was just with him two weeks ago on the Annual Bike Ride. He was such a nice guy! Do you know what happened?

Dan: I have no idea. All I know is that he was in the bedroom and couldn't get out. He died in the fire. His wife and step-son got out. We've been friends since college. I brought him into the company. I'm just so upset, I've got to go, I'll call you later.

Jan sat there, stunned. It was tragic. What to do? This was the first (and hopefully only) loss of an employee she had ever dealt with. Jan called her CEO because she knew that the CEO would want to know, especially since Ed was one of the top salespeople in his region. She was able to get him right away. He was as devastated as she and Dan were. While they were talking, they both started googling the news for the city where Ed lived to find out more. Nothing. They agreed to stay in touch, and Jan began to work on a communication to the sales team and tried to contact the family.

Jan was quite upset but able to get the emergency contact number for Ed's wife. Jan got Ed's wife's dad on the phone, who explained they were at the house with the fire marshal. He thanked her for calling, took down her name and number and said his daughter would call back.

About an hour later, Jan got a call from Ed's wife. As they talked, Jan was perplexed by how calm Ed's wife was. Jan felt even more confused when the conversation turned to life insurance; the woman's husband wasn't even dead a full twenty-four hours and the house was still smoldering! Jan promised to get back to her by Monday with the answers to all of her questions. When Ed's wife handed the phone back to her dad, he thanked Jan for being available on a Saturday.

Jan received a number of calls throughout the day, all from people equally sad when they learned of Ed's death. She also spent some time online to learn more about the fire. There was still nothing on the news. Ed's friends rallied and ordered "Remember Ed" wristbands to be given to all at the annual sales conference the company was hosting that week.

As the week progressed, serious suspicions about Ed's final hours began surfacing. Rumors were rampant that this was no accidental fire. Members of Ed's local team and some of the executive team left the conference early to attend Ed's funeral. The feedback was that the atmosphere was "weird." Jan was told that Ed's family and friends stayed on one side of the room, while his wife and her family stayed on the other side, and none of them spoke to each other.

Within two weeks of Ed's death, the cause of the fire was declared "intentional" and it emerged that his wife and her boyfriend had been charged with murder, felony murder, and first-degree arson. The medical examiner put Ed's death down to a combination of smoke inhalation and thermal burns. It was alleged that while Ed was asleep in the master bedroom, his wife had set the fire, and he was unable to get out. Both of the accused were being held without bail.

Over the ensuing months, there were numerous conversations between the investigators, Ed's friends, coworkers, and of course, HR. Ed's family remained in close touch with HR, as life insurance and other benefits were in limbo pending the trial.

Sixteen months after Ed's death, the trial came to an end. On Ed's birthday, the jury came back and found his wife guilty on all three counts, and she was sentenced to life plus twenty years. She did not appeal the verdict or sentence. On the other hand, her boyfriend was found not guilty on all counts because the prosecutor was unable to connect him, since he was not in the area at the time of the fire. He had been in jail for over fourteen months awaiting trial.

The moral of the story: Ed was an excellent salesperson and loved by all at work. However, the stories about his life and relationship with his wife that came out at trial made it clear that you never know what anyone is dealing with outside of the office. There's a quote that I refer to often "Be kind to everyone; we are all fighting our own battles." Most people have something going on in their life that work gives them some respite from dealing with. It's not as important to know the details of what others are dealing with as it to intuitively know that things are generally not what they seem, and a simple smile or act of kindness can do more for a colleague than you might ever know.

MURDER, HE WROTE

"Hello, Jan. How are you? This is Fred. I need your help with something."

Jan (HR): Hi Fred! It's nice to hear from you. How can I assist?

Fred (Manager): I have not heard from Becky in several days. It is not like her. She always lets me know when she'll be out or late. I've been calling her cell, but it goes straight to voicemail. She is not answering her home phone either. I'm not sure what to do, and I have clients wondering when the work will get done.

Jan: I haven't seen Becky in the office lately either. Let me look up her emergency contact information and see what I can find out. I'll call you back shortly.

Jan proceeded to pull up the information from the HR system and found a number for Becky's adult son. She called him, and it was a very strange conversation. Becky's son seemed unconcerned and said he didn't have a car or the money for a cab to go check on her. He didn't know any of the neighbors, so there was little he could do. If he heard from his mom, he'd let Jan know. Well, that was not the answer she was hoping for!

Jan made a split-second decision to call the police because, she thought, *You just never know.* She provided the dispatcher with Becky's information and told him that it had been more than three days since she stopped communicating. The dispatcher told Jan he would send a patrol car over to the home and call back.

About an hour later, Jan received a shocking call. The officer had gone to the front door and got no response. He went to the rear door and saw someone lying on the floor. He had to force his way in and found Becky motionless with no heart beat. He called for back-up and medical support, but Becky was declared dead at the scene. It was later learned that she had been dead at least three days and had died from a severe beating and asphyxiation. Her car was missing.

After numerous interviews with family and friends, an all-points bulletin was put out for her estranged boyfriend, who was twenty-two years her junior. He was picked up driving her car and did not resist arrest. The police charged him with first-degree murder. It seems they'd had a tumultuous relationship for a few years and, on the night of her death, according to the records, they had been smoking crack cocaine and drinking heavily when a fight ensued. Her son stated this was not unusual. In this case, drugs and alcohol certainly were a recipe for disaster.

After a brief trial, in which the boyfriend took an Alford plea (allowing the defendant to plead guilty without offering specifics of the crime), he was sentenced to thirty years in prison. There were no winners but a lot of losers in this case. She left behind three children and several sisters.

People at the office asked themselves, *Why didn't I know?* This employee did a great job with clients and she was well liked. But Becky is another reminder that you really don't know the person sitting right next to you. There was never an opportunity to lend a hand or an ear, or offer assistance of any kind, and colleagues were left wondering if they could have done anything to help her. While the crime took place outside of work and off hours, the impact on those she worked with was deep and wide.

Becky's work colleagues received calls from her family members seeking help with funeral costs because no one in the family could afford to bury her. Can you just imagine how that made fellow employees feel? And Jan had to talk with the funeral home and provide life-insurance information. Of course, until the investigation was completed, the insurance company would not release any funds from the life policy, as they had to be sure that no one in the family named as a beneficiary was involved.

It was a very emotional time within the company because it had only been three months since the company had lost Ed, a salesperson, who had been murdered by his wife. Poor Jan had to handle both instances, and she had not been with the company long. She wondered what kind of company had she joined!

MURDER, HE WROTE ... AGAIN

HR received a call that one of the top employees had called his boss to say he would be out indefinitely because his brother had murdered his wife and was on the run from the police!

When the guy finally returned to work, he was really not able to function or concentrate. Of course, his work suffered, his marriage suffered, and he finally had to depart the business. A major loss all around for all connected to this tragedy.

He lost his sister-in-law, his brother, his wife, and his job. Fortunately, in recent times, it appears he has recovered, but it was quite tough going for a long period of time for this person.

THE REVEREND

This is a sad story about the impact of domestic violence and a woman trapped in a relationship with a person who had great power over her. Unfortunately, it affected the business where she worked, and given that domestic violence infiltrates the workplace in the most heinous ways, the organization had to act to protect the wider employee population.

Clare would come to work periodically with bruises, abrasions, and cuts. She was either quite clumsy or there was something more going on. On one particular day, she arrived clearly distraught and bearing visible injuries to her face. At the urging of a colleague, she finally revealed that her boyfriend was physically and verbally abusing her and that she did not know how to get away from him. The coworker encouraged her to seek assistance from HR, as it was impacting her ability to do her job, which could be a threat to her continued employment.

When she met with Gail in HR she broke down, telling her everything. She had been with this guy for quite some time, but after the initial courtship, the relationship turned abusive. The boyfriend wanted to know everywhere she went and who she had been speaking to. He checked her phone regularly, and he followed her places. He timed her visits to the store, he timed her drive home from the office, and she had to answer to him constantly. She feared going home as much as she feared not going home. Recently, he had begun following her to the office to make sure she went to work and also coming to the office again at the end of the day to make sure she drove straight home.

Gail asked Clare what her boyfriend did for a living that allowed him the flexibility to stalk her. To Gail's surprise, she learned he was a reverend at a local church. It was a new church, which the reverend had started himself, and it had grown over the past five years.

Gail asked Clare what she could do to assist. She gave Clare information about the Employee Assistance Program (EAP) and strongly encouraged her to call the number to get some professional help. Clare was crying and shaking; she was definitely afraid to make the call from her cell phone and did not want to call from her desk. Gail offered to leave the room and give her space to make the call, if she wanted to do it right away. Clare was grateful and made the call.

When she came out of the office, she looked a little relieved and told Gail that she had some thinking to do. The EAP consultant had encouraged her to make a decision to keep herself safe. She had her own apartment and paid all of her own expenses, so all she needed to do was figure out how to keep him from entering her apartment without making him angry. She needed some space and the ability to think. Gail encouraged her to take some time and get her life sorted; since she had personal time off (PTO) on the books, why not make use of this benefit? The employee replied, "How would I explain my taking time off to him? He'd insist on being with me to keep track of me."

She had an excellent point. She and Gail brainstormed some solutions. She disclosed that she wanted him out of her life. How could she make that happen? Because she had been physically abused, a law had been broken, so she could seek legal advice; however, at that suggestion she really looked scared. They talked about going to a women's refuge. But at this point, Gail had entered a "danger zone" for a HR professional whose job is not to give this kind of advice because it could backfire on HR and the business. HR can provide resources but not personal advice, which steps outside of the boundaries.

Clare left HR with the plan to take the rest of the day off and consider her options. But when she got to her car, she found that her tires had been slashed! Coincidence? Probably not. She called the police from her cell phone, and before the police arrived, the reverend showed up. How did he know that the tires had been slashed and that she was leaving the office early? He offered no explanation and denied slashing the tires. The police arrived, took the report, and departed. She couldn't mention her suspicions about the reverend to them because he was right there. The rest of the afternoon was spent with AAA and getting her car drivable again so she could get home. So much for figuring out options and making a plan.

The next day, Clare reported to HR that it was another sleepless night for her. During the lunch hour, a few employees told her they had noticed that the trunk of her car was open and the alarm was going off. The reverend was seen in the parking lot, and he took off when he realized he had been spotted. That really unnerved her. It also unnerved the employees.

Another trip to HR. Gail determined that this is now a potential safety issue and called in the building facilities manager, but she was told that this was a police issue and the building's management would not provide a security service. However, since the building facilities manager was aware that a car's tires had been slashed the day before, he decided to call the police and let them know what was going on.

The police arrived and approached the reverend. He had a viable excuse: He was making sure that his girlfriend's car was not the subject of another attack of vandalism like it had been the day before! That seemed quite logical to them, so they departed again. That night, the employee was subjected to more physical abuse. He accused her of calling the police on him. How dare she do that! What kind of a girlfriend would call the police on her boyfriend? When she arrived at the office the next day, she had a black eye, and her wrist was wrapped. She went to the HR office and asked if she could use the phone again.

This time, she called the police and asked how she could put a restraining order on someone. She was told she had to go to the district court and do it in person in front of a judge. How was she going to do that knowing that he was watching her car in the parking lot? She began to cry and shake; it seemed to be hopeless. Gail decided to place a call to the company's general counsel office. After going through the whole story, she was advised that action needed to be taken for the safety of all employees. They are now on notice of a potential problem that could endanger the larger population and precautionary measures needed to be taken.

Gail was instructed to tell Clare that she would need to find a way to get the restraining order in place, and that she will need to work from home for the short term. The company would also have to hire a temporary security company to monitor the parking lot for signs of the reverend.

The employee agreed to the plan and was able to get a family member to take her to the courthouse. The restraining order was served that evening. The reverend was actually at her apartment when the sheriff arrived and ordered him to vacate immediately. The sheriff told Gail by phone the next day that it was not a pretty scene. While he went peacefully in front of the sheriff, he was heard to mutter, "You'll be sorry" as he departed. Gail would work from home the rest of that week and planned to return to the office the following week, once she was confidant he was complying with the order. It was agreed that she would keep Gail informed.

Things seemed to go along pretty well for a short time. The employee was coming to work on time; the ex-boyfriend was not to be found anywhere near the business, and no new injuries were sighted. Well, that didn't last too long. A few short weeks later, the employee confided to a coworker that she was trying to reconcile with the reverend. He had been calling her and begging her to come back to him. She had been out with a few girlfriends recently when he showed up at the bar and was so nice to her. Her girlfriends were uncomfortable and suggested it was time to go. She went with them. He followed her home but did not come into the apartment parking lot; he said he was just making sure she was safe.

She confided that she was confused and lonely. She knew how nice he could be, remembering their courtship before things got ugly. The night before he had begged her to let him come over. She agreed and broke the restraining order! She told her colleague she wanted to cancel the restraining order. Maybe she'd jumped too quickly and could have done something different?

The employee was furious with her! She told her that she was taking a huge risk with her job and putting her coworkers at risk. She told Clare that the women in the department had been afraid of the reverend, and because they didn't know what he was capable of, she was going to let HR know. Clare begged her not to say anything, but it was no use. HR was notified.

Of course, once the pair were reconciled, it didn't take long for the reverend to go back to his old ways. One night, he came by her home after work and was being very nice, so she asked him to stay for dinner. Things got physical and he gave her a black eye. She called the police and they arrested him, and there was to be a court hearing at 9:30 the following morning. Because HR was aware that he had told Clare in the past that he would kill her if she ever had him arrested, the company had to call security back in, just in case he was released by the court and came back to find Clare at the office.

Gail put in another call to general counsel. After many conversations about the best interests of the larger population, it was determined that the risk to employee safety was too great; this guy was a loose cannon. Clare had to make a choice and she chose to resign. She shunned all of the available resources and went back to the reverend because his power over her was too great. Gail was sad and the team was sad, but the reality is that not everyone can be helped.

BRIBERY

An email came into the HR leader alleging an unethical situation. It seems that a sales-support employee was seeking cash payments from salespeople whom he was employed to support. The payments were to be made from the net pay of those folks and to be outside of payroll. Apparently, this setup had been going on for years, but a newly hired outside salesperson on the team felt he was getting the "shake-down," and if he didn't comply, he would be at the bottom of the list for sales support help!

The HR leader contacted one of the tenured members on the team to look into the situation. He asked HR if he could handle it "generically" and not make a big deal out of it. He wanted to simply send a notice out that this was not only against company policy but also against state and federal payroll laws.

While that was a good option, HR also felt that the employee who was doing the "shaking down" also needed a one-on-one conversation so that the complainant would not be ostracized from the team and would have the same support as everyone else.

Well, as you might imagine, that conversation did not go well. Evidently, the sales-support employees had a very good thing going and were earning significant "under the table" compensation from the folks they supported. No wonder there was no turnover on that team! The employee under investigation became belligerent and hostile with the HR person. Eventually, he calmed down but let it be known that he disagreed with the decision and would be seeking employment elsewhere.

This really upset the tenured sales folks because they received great service from this person. But, the feeling of the manager was that if he chose to leave, the company would look for a replacement who did not require bribes in order to do the job.

JUST ANOTHER DAY IN SALES

The sales leader in this story is a real comedian, and he had the place laughing out loud through the retelling of this experience.

The sales leader was in a meeting at a client site. An employee of the client entered the conference room and told the attendees that no one was allowed to leave the building because there was a black bear in the parking lot! The meeting was being held at a location not known for black bears, so they waited until the coast was clear.

Finally able to depart, the sales leader headed to New York City for his next appointment. He was driving along while participating on a conference call, but when he turned a corner, his phone slid off the center console. He reached to pick it up and was spotted by a traffic officer. Of course, he got pulled over. He tried to explain to the officer that he had not been using the phone, he had simply been retrieving it. At that moment, he told the folks on the conference call that he needed to go and he'd talk to them again later.

The normal routine ensued, and he gave the police officer his driver's license, registration, and insurance card. The officer went to his patrol car and the sales leader waited, expecting to get a simple warning so he could be off. The officer returned and asks him to get out of the car. "Why?" he demanded. "Please just step out of the car, sir," the officer replied. The sales leader complied and was immediately handcuffed and walked to the back of the patrol car!

As he sat there listening to the two officers chat, he finally said, "Excuse me, can you tell me why I am in handcuffs?" To which one officer responded, "Your driving privileges have been revoked in New York City."

"What are you talking about? I've been driving here for years!" replied the sales leader.

"Sir, a notice was sent to your address in New Jersey."

"I haven't lived at that address since I was nineteen years old!"

The sales leader was in his forties at this point. In addition to his confusion, he was starting to worry about his baby, his 5-series BMW that he would not be allowed to drive away in. He commented to the quite young officer about his concern, and the officer replied, "Maybe I could drive the car for you!"

When there is a handcuffed person in the patrol car, two patrol officers must be in the car for safety purposes. However, they were able to work it out so that the young officer could drive the car to the station by calling in a "reinforcement" to ride in the car with his partner and prisoner. Off they go to the tenth precinct to process this hardened criminal.

At the station, the sales leader was put in a holding cell. He had to turn in his property, including his cell phone, which made him feel stripped and naked because his cell phone was never more than ten feet away from him—he was a die-hard deal maker! After a few minutes, the officers came back with a coke, which he drank despite not having had a coke in more than five years (desperate times call for desperate measures), but they also handed him a miracle: his cell phone!

He finally learned that he had received a speeding ticket in 1989 that he had never paid or appeared in court for. The police asked him if he remembered getting that ticket. "I was a senior in high school, of course I don't remember that!" he said. After a mug shot, fingerprints, and a $250 fine, he was released but not allowed to drive in the city yet.

He called one of his sales guys and asked him to take the subway to the tenth precinct. He needed someone to drive him and his car out of there! The employee was rolling with laughter and thought about leaving his boss there for a while longer, but he complied and rescued him. This was a typical day in the life of this very fun and successful sales leader. I always loved getting his calls as they usually started with "You are not going to believe this…"

NOT SO FAST ...

A sales leader and a few of his direct reports, some of whom happened to be related to each other, decided collectively to leave the company and go to another company. While this happens quite often, there's a legal way to do it and a not-so-legal way to do it. This is a story of the latter.

Generally speaking, people have a "right to work" in most states and a company cannot hold you hostage by a non-compete contract clause. However, they can (and most do) hold you to a non-solicitation clause that prohibits you from poaching employees and clients for a period of time. In addition, employees are not to take confidential company information with them to the next company. This would include client lists, client contact information, contracts, pricing sheets, financials, and so on. Doing so could land you with a lawsuit seeking injunctive relief and other damages. Not too smart.

Well, this group wasn't too smart. About two weeks prior to giving their notice, the sales leader sent a note out to the sales staff asking each of them to forward their client database to him so he could "consolidate them into one database." This guy not only asked once, he asked three times! First at 7:33 a.m. on one day, then the next day at 9:23 a.m., and on the third day at 8:16 a.m. The final time the note read: "To date I have made two requests for your account database and have received one file from Don. I am no longer asking for this information—I am telling you to get it to me. This is the last email on the subject. If you can't figure out how to export your file or copy it to me, print a hard copy and I will have it re-entered into the consolidated database."

Three days later, he must have received what he wanted as he sent the client list (and a few other documents that contained confidential client contracts with pricing) from his work email to his home email. They all gave their notice two days after the home email was sent. Indefensible!

So, the former employer filed a suit, won the injunction, and the employee was not able to communicate with the clients contained in the documents, making them less valuable to the new company for a period of time. The only winners here were the attorneys on both sides, as always.

ADJUSTER FRAUD

One of the roles of a property claims manager at an insurance firm is to complete random file audits as part of an insurance adjuster's annual performance review. The process is to pull a number of closed claims, review the content of the files, and call the parties to the claim to inquire about customer service and to verify the payments made were actually received by the insured homeowner.

On one such occasion, the claims manager called the policyholder. She was quite nice and appreciative of the prompt, courteous service. Her basement had experienced a flood, and all repairs had been made and personal items replaced to her satisfaction. She had no complaints and would recommend the insurance carrier to anyone, especially given the great claims service she had received. She was also appreciative of the follow-up call by the claims manager.

When the claims manager inquired about the initial payment and the need for the supplement payment that had been issued, the homeowner innocently responded that there had been no supplemental payment to her knowledge. She agreed to double check with her husband and call the claims manager back. The file was set aside for the moment. The following day, as promised, the policyholder called the claims manager back and advised that there was only one check issued. It was payable to them and to the contractor.

Interesting, the second check was only made payable to the contractor, according to the file copy.

The next call was to the contractor. After a few messages had not been returned, the claims manager did a search for all checks that had been issued with this contractor's name. There were a large number and, the same adjuster had issued each! Hmmm. One last strongly worded voicemail to the contractor finally resulted in a return call.

He did not want to talk on the phone and agreed to meet for coffee halfway between their two offices. They met the following day. The claims manager brought the file in question along with the long list of payments made to the contractor.

He considered himself very professional and stated that he was going to come clean. Evidently, the adjuster and he had become "chums" over the years. No romantic involvement, just friends. She had come to him about eight months prior because she and her husband were having financial problems. She needed his help but would understand if he couldn't or wouldn't do it for her. They devised a scheme wherein he would be the contractor she recommended, she would issue the first check to him and the named insured, but then she would issue a second check to him against a supplemental estimate. He would cash the check and give her all the proceeds. He did not take any of the money; he was simply trying to help a friend get out of a bind. He said he had no idea how many checks or how much was involved! He said he only did it a few times.

The evidence reflected close to $15,000 in insurance fraud through these supplemental checks. The most interesting part of this is that he was a full-time police officer in a major city and his contracting business earned extra income for his family. He was quite concerned about what was going to happen to him now that he had been "caught." The claims manager advised him that it was a legal matter, as it would need to be reported to the police once the employee had been dealt with. He was asked not to let the employee know what was going on; it would be better for him if he cooperated with the investigation. He agreed, and they parted ways.

The claims manager returned to the office and set up a meeting with the director of claims and the director of legal along with the HR leader. All agreed there was enough evidence to terminate employment. The employee was invited to come in the following morning for her annual performance review.

Upon arrival at the claims manager's office, she was surprised to see the claims director. The conversation went something like this:

Claims Manager: Good morning. The claims director is here as part of my annual review, I hope you are okay with that.

Adjuster: Of course, no problem. Nice to see we all get treated the same with performance reviews!

Claims Manager: Before we go over the actual review, let's take a look at the files that I reviewed, please feel free to comment as we go along.

So they started going through the files and by about the fifth file, the claims manager noticed the adjuster's hands shaking.

Claims Manager: Are you okay?

Adjuster: Yes.

Claims Manager: Do you notice anything unusual about the files?

Adjuster: No.

The manager decided to just get it over with.

Claims Manager: It seems that each of these files have the same contractor and each of these files have a supplemental payment to the contractor that did not include the insured's name as a payee. Why is that?

The adjuster simply shrugged her shoulders.

Claims Manager: What would you think if I told you I have spoken with the contractor about this? What do you think the contractor told me?

Again, a simple shrug and the adjuster would not look up.

Claims Manager: Look, it appears to me and to my director here that you have played the system to your own gain. I am told by the contractor that you are having some financial challenges and you two agreed to scheme the system with issuing false supplemental invoices. We have found at least $15,000 of fraudulent claims so far. How much more will we find?

The adjuster started crying and said she wasn't sure. She was quite distraught.

Claims Manager: Obviously, your employment here is now done. I need your key cards, your credit card, and the company car turned over now.

The hardest part of this for the manager was that the adjuster had no way to get home. It was decided that the manager would drive her home. That was quite disconcerting to the manager, who really didn't want to drive in the same car with her. Well, as it turned out, when they arrived at the adjuster's home, she opened the garage door and inside was a lot of claims salvage that she had taken possession of, stuff that she had indicated in the claim file had no salvage value and had been destroyed! She was also selling the salvage and keeping that money!

The next day, the claims manager went to the police station for the jurisdiction where the adjuster lived to report the fraud. She was told that they would take the report, but it was a tough county that was dealing with significant drug crime and homicides, so they had no real time to deal with white-collar crime. They were pretty sure that she and the contractor would be charged, but they doubted that the district attorney would bother doing much because they were overloaded with criminal cases. A mere $15,000 fraud from a very large insurance company would get little to no attention.

The claims manager still wanted her charged. The police agreed and said they'd be in touch. The woman was charged, agreed to restitution but never made a payment. A judgment against her was filed and that was the end of that. As for the police officer, he was charged and lost his job but kept his contracting business. As he did not financially benefit, no judgment could be placed against him, but he now had a criminal record that was basically just a slap on the wrist. Who says crime doesn't pay?

D.C. DRUG BUST

This really happened to me back in the old insurance claim days.

Myself and another claims adjuster had two property claims to inspect in Washington D.C. Neither location was in a place that was necessarily safe for male adjusters, much less young female adjusters. My coworker, who has since become a very good friend, probably has the largest, most beautiful eyes of anyone I have ever met, and we decided to tag team the inspections to feel safer and drive to both locations together. At that time, we were all issued brand new Chrysler Aries K as our company car. She offered to drive, and we headed out to my location first in northeast D.C. It was a commercial business that had suffered a water loss.

While I was inside gathering the claims information from the business owner, I heard someone in the office scream, "Everyone get down on the floor!" The employees hit the floor and called for me to get down too. I had no idea what was going on but laid on the floor on my stomach like the others. They started whispering among themselves that it was another drug raid outside! After a few minutes, one of the employees poked their head up and peered outside. He said it looks like it's under control and we could look out.

Very carefully, I crawled to the window. I was two stories above the ground and looked down to see police everywhere, some in uniform and some in plain clothes. Up against the ten-foot chain link fence were quite a few men in various forms of undress (they evidently wore layers and start stripping while running from the police so that the "last seen wearing..." reports were not accurate!). They had their fingers curled in the chain link fence and were "spread eagle," not moving or flinching, watched by police officers with very large guns. More suspects were being caught and walked to the fence to be frisked. I had never seen anything like this except on TV police shows!

I scanned the area looking for my colleague who had stayed in the car waiting for me. I saw her quite a distance away, and all I could see was the whites of her very large, beautiful eyes that were as big as saucers! This was in the early stages of car phones, and I was able to call her to make sure she was okay. She was in the middle of the raid with officers running and chasing drug suspects. She was fine but wanted to get the heck out of there as quickly as possible! I told her to start making her way towards the building as I was heading out.

As I left the property, I told the owner that I would not be back, all further communications would be done via phone and mail! He understood and thanked me for coming by. Of course, I had to let the underwriting department know that this insured location was in an undesirable address and there was definitely a risk of future losses!

My friend and I still talk about that day. While it was quite scary at the time, it has provided a lot of laughs as we reflect back on the craziness of watching these men running past her, while stripping down layers, and officers screaming "halt or I'll shoot," and watching the criminals get frisked. What an experience! But one that I never wanted to repeat, and neither did my colleague!

CLAIMS MASTURBATION

This particular incident really challenged me as a relatively new property claims manager.

I was sitting at my desk and received a call from one of my direct reports that their coworker had not been in the office for a few days. I tried to call the adjuster and could not reach him. Several attempts throughout the day were made to no avail. Coincidentally, I also received calls from two policyholders that they had not heard from this adjuster since their new claim had been assigned to him. This was really starting to get concerning and quite mysterious.

The next morning, I drove to the adjuster's office and found an absolute mess! There were several days of new claims on his desk, untouched. A stack of mail unopened made it quite clear that he had not been around for quite some time, at least a week! I put in a call to his house, and his wife answered the phone. She was very vague about his whereabouts and said that when she heard from him, she would have him call me. I had attended their wedding a few years before, so I was quite surprised by her tone and demeanor with me on the phone.

Late in the day, he finally called me. He sounded quite anxious and not himself. I first wanted to know if he was okay, especially from a health standpoint. He said he was fine, he was going through some very tough family issues and he should have called me. He went on to say that he

had not been working and that I could charge him leave. He still needed a few more days off, but he did intend to come back to work. I kept prodding for some answers as this was so unlike him; he had been a good employee for nearly five years!

Finally, he said that he had been arrested the week before and that had led to some significant challenges with his wife. He did not want to talk about it. I asked him when and where he had been arrested. Again, he vaguely described that it had been around 4:00 p.m. on a Wednesday at a local university. I advised him that he needed to tell me what was going on because that incident, whatever it was, would have taken place during work hours. Was he in the company car? Yes. He again refused to go into any details. I told him to rethink his response and that we needed to talk again the following day. At that point, I needed to figure out the claims mess he had left me. I also told him that I would need to speak with my boss, as this could have future employment implications. That really upset him, and he reiterated that what he had done had nothing to do with the company! But I knew there was a problem, since it involved the company car and it happened during work hours.

It took me until nearly 8:00 p.m. to get through the mess on his desk, reassigning the new claims, organizing the mail, and so on. It was a challenge that could have been avoided if only he had called me right after whatever happened! His coworkers were concerned about him and also frustrated since they now had to pick up the slack he created.

The next morning I spoke with my director. He pushed me hard to find out what happened, especially since the company car was involved. We brainstormed and decided that while the adjuster had "forbidden" me to do any research on what happened as it was a personal matter and not job related, I needed to do some digging. We got the green light from corporate legal.

I headed to the local courthouse for the jurisdiction where the university was to see if I could find an arrest document in the court system.

WOW! I could not believe what I was reading. The arrest warrant stated the charges of indecent exposure on the college campus. According to the documents, he had used the company car to slowly follow young women. As he approached them, he was not only exposing himself but also masturbating as he drove slowly alongside them. When the young student realized what he was doing, she would take off. He would then look for his next prey. The charging document stated there were three separate instances reported within a forty-five minute period!

He was not too bright, it seemed, because a campus policeman pulled up behind him at a stop sign, and the employee was obviously not paying attention to what was going on behind him. The policeman got out of his car, walked up, and caught him "red handed." He was arrested, the car was impounded, and he was taken into the county police (college campus police have no arresting authority; they are the "middlemen" when it comes to actual arrest warrants), where he was charged, booked, and released to his wife.

Although you are innocent until proven guilty by a court of law, from an employment perspective, the guy had to go. First of all, he did not have any claims on the university campus, so what was he doing there during work hours in a company car? He had been AWOL for several days, during which time he had left the policyholders hanging, and he "exposed" the company to possible legal liability, given that the car was registered to the company and not to him! Any of the victims could have considered a lawsuit, and while it would be a challenge for them to win, it would still have had litigation and reputation costs to the company.

Once I returned to the office with copies of the charges, I met with my director and the chief counsel. We agreed that termination was in order, and I placed a call to the employee advising him that he needed to be in the office that afternoon, no excuses. When he arrived, I went through what I had learned, and can you believe how angry he was that I had "meddled" in his personal life? He told me I had no right to go to the courthouse after he had explicitly told me not to! He continued to rant about how this had nothing to do with his job, and it was punishment enough that he had suffered through trying to save his marriage without losing his job too.

This was a total misunderstanding, he said, and he would be found not guilty; he felt confident about that. He still could not explain why he was on the university campus rather than working his claims. He tried to explain that as a field adjuster, he did not have to account for his time and whereabouts every day. I let him get most of the anger out of his system and then calmly asked him for his car keys, building keys, ID badge, and so on. I then escorted him out, wishing him luck with his court case.

EPILOGUE: He was found guilty by a judge and put on two years probation and prohibited from being on the campus. Sadly, it was also his alma mater.

JUVENILE FELON

An employee who had been working for several years was sent to a new job site that required very stringent background checks. Evidently, this was a very talented employee who was in demand for his skills.

The client let the employer know that the background check revealed this employee was a convicted felon. They wondered if the social security number was off, or if it was a case of stolen identity or some other mix-up. When HR contacted the employee, he was quite surprised by the questions because, in fact, he had been charged with four felonies as a juvenile before he turned sixteen years old. He had been convicted of a major heist along with a few others, taken from his family home, and sent to a juvenile facility while he awaited trial.

After he was convicted, he spent his teenage years in juvenile detention and was later released to a group home to learn life skills before finally being freed at the age of eighteen. He said that he now followed strict rules as he did not want to spend his life incarcerated. He had a child almost as soon as he got out of prison, and he realized that he did not want the life he had led thus far for his child.

His explanation was that he got in with the wrong crowd at a very young age and did some really dumb things. He thought and had been told that once he completed his three years of subsequent probation that his record was to be sealed and then he could get the record expunged.

HR explained to him that his record came up with the background check by the client. Why did he indicate on his application that he had not been convicted of a crime? He again emphasized that his attorney had advised that his record should be clear and that he did not need to disclose because it had been more than seven years since his release, and he had served his time. Well, the record was still out there for all to see, and he would need to get this cleared up.

After discussing with legal, it was determined that he was under no obligation to disclose what should have been an expunged record, he had been an excellent employee for several years and the client wanted to keep him on site. You just never know when your past could come back to haunt you!

LEWD FELON

A manager went to HR stating that he had received a call from a client asking if an employee on site was a convicted felon. HR had no idea. This would need to be checked out.

After a very quick Google search, there the employee was, photo and all! The charge involved an illegal sexual act with a minor under the age of fourteen by force or fear. A decision had to be made about what to do because the client did not want this person on the premises.

This employee had come over with an acquisition of another company. A review of the employment application showed he had responded yes to the "have you ever been convicted of a felony" question with a comment to speak with him privately. A quick call to the HR team revealed that a background check had not been done because the crime happened many, many years ago and it was felt he had served his time. The company agreed to bring him on as he had excellent skills that were needed.

The error made here was that the client had very strict policies on past legal violations and the company did a poor job of assigning him to client sites. All of this could have been avoided, and his coworker did not have to be involved, if the company had handled this problem more discreetly. It all goes to show that you just never know the full story of the person working alongside you.

CAYMAN BANKING

I'm sure many folks have read about or know of the benefits of banking in the Cayman Islands. But I doubt many of you ever thought about opening an account there with someone else's money, like your company's money!

That is exactly what one employee did to a small company. She was the signatory on the accounts, which were not consistently audited, so she became quite skilled at writing checks and having them deposited to an account in the Caymans. I have no idea how this worked, but it was discovered that this employee had written a number of checks over a period, and by the time it was discovered, $50,000 was sitting in an account that didn't belong to the company in the beautiful Cayman Islands!

Needless to say, she was fired. However, the police in both the United States and the Cayman Islands refused to prosecute, so she got away with the money-laundering scheme. It's unbelievable that white-collar crime must involve hundreds of thousand of dollars before legal action can be taken. There are just too many violent, serious criminals for law enforcement to be bothered.

PISTOL WHIPPED

A sales leader knew his days were numbered after both his sales manager and the CEO told him they did not have the confidence that he could get the job done in his territory. When the office manager came into work the following morning, she did her normal walk around the office to make sure all was in order before the day started. Imagine her surprise when she checked the boss's office and found that his desktop computer had been shot up with bullets!

She didn't know what to do and called HR (of course, doesn't everyone call HR when they don't know what to do?) to let them know. They in turn called the sales leader, but of course he had no clue what happened. He said he'd come right in to check it out.

"Good, because we've called the police, and I'm sure they'll want to chat with you." Well, you can imagine he was a no show at the office after hearing that! When questioned by the police, he had no knowledge. His tenure was ended that day, a few days early, but the company was done with him.

Why can't people just leave quietly?

BULLIES & BLOWHARDS

TATTOO

It was time for the annual executive strategic planning meeting. The CEO decided to expose some next-level leaders to the process and invited two vice presidents who would not normally attend. This was an off-site meeting, and in all, there were about eleven leaders in attendance. At the end of the day, there was the obligatory dinner. Everyone was enjoying a nice dinner with appropriate banter back and forth as they shared personal and professional stories.

One of the invited guests came up with a game that she wanted to play. Everyone was asked to put $20 in the center of the table and then guess how many tattoos were "represented" at the table. In other words, we were each to look around the table and first guess if the person had one or more tattoos, and then how many tattoos in total the group had. If you had a tattoo, you were required to disclose.

The head of HR was appalled that this game was suggested and the CEO did not object and was having fun with the idea! But the head of HR did not object because she was really hoping that he would speak up.

As it turned out, the head of HR was the only person with a tattoo, and she felt she had to disclose because integrity was very important to her. Of course, once she disclosed, there was shock, followed by questions about what kind of tattoo, where the tattoo was, and what the story behind it was.

The woman simply stated that she did not want to talk about it any further and they quickly moved on.

During the next one-on-one conversation with her boss (the CEO), the head of HR let him know how very disappointed she was that he did not put a stop to the game when it was initially announced. He was understanding and concurred that it was his responsibility to speak up; he just wasn't thinking because he got caught up in the frivolity. He agreed that it was inappropriate and offered to call the person who had suggested the game. She thanked him but said he didn't need to make a huge case out of it. She accepted his apology and accountability for the incident.

There were lessons learned by both the CEO and HR leader. She realized she needed to speak up when things weren't right at the time they are happening. He understood that he needed to remain in control and speak up when social events get too personal and employees are about to get carried away. And the lesson for readers of this book is that no matter where you are or who you are with, you have a duty to act and to speak up—if not for yourself, for the others who are unable to speak for themselves.

MY IP

This is a story of one employee who was saved from termination, but then—after learning a lot about the business—tried to throw his weight around. It backfired.

The HR leader was alone in the office during lunch. The printer went off and began printing numerous pages. HR had a confidential printer that only HR team members could use (a special IP address had been set up by IT).

Curious, the HR leader walked over to the printer. Lo and behold, the printer was spewing pages of pornographic photos! *How can this happen?* she thought. She actually started shaking, and her mind was racing about what to do. She went to her boss, the CFO, and told him what had happened. They were both quite perplexed, so they contacted the IT department to see if they could figure it out.

The first response was that it was impossible to know who was printing the images. The HR leader pushed harder until they took the time to review the printer data. They found that the photos were being printed from a repurposed laptop, formerly belonging to an HR employee but now in the possession of another employee in a nearby office.

The CFO and the HR leader decided that the employee would be brought in for questioning the next day. Off she drove to meet with him and his boss. He was shocked when she showed him the photos and explained how they were connected back to his laptop. The story he gave is hysterical now, but it was not at that time. He said he had been playing around on the internet the night before and had visited some sites. He thought he was printing to his home printer but nothing came out so he gave up. He also stated that two of the photos were of his mom and stepdad at a nude beach. . . now who would even admit that? This was his first job out of school, and he had a lot to learn. The HR leader explained the company's Electronic Use Policy and that, even though he was at home on his own time, he was using the company equipment against company policy. If he wanted to visit these sites, he must use his own equipment!

The next day, the CFO wanted to make sure the new employee knew how serious this was and paid him a visit as well to offer some additional coaching. He got off quite easy with a simple verbal warning!

FAST FORWARD about four years. The porno peeper had achieved some career progression and was running a small team. He kept trying to convince the COO that his team was underpaid for the work they were doing. There had been some issues with his team along the way, and it appeared that he was building a union-type mentality. The COO asked him to put together a business plan for how his team would deliver value to the client and to the business. Two weeks passed and nothing. He returned to the COO requesting compensation consideration for his team. "Where's the business plan I asked for?" said the COO.

"If I give you a business plan, I'd be giving up my personal intellectual property," he said. He would not do that unless the COO immediately gave him and each member of his team a 25 percent increase in pay! "If we don't get the increase," he added, "we'll probably leave, and you will not be able to deliver the project to the client."

The COO was holding back his temper! Four years ago, this guy was given a chance to build a career, and now he wants to hold the company hostage? The COO kept his cool and let him know that he had personally given a lot of his time to coach the employee and help him grow. He advised the employee to think about a few things. First, he needed to disassociate his compensation from what is to be delivered by his team to the client. If he believed that he and his team were under-compensated, then he needed to do the work on the business case so that it could be reviewed and acted upon in the proper manner.

The employee then went out on a two-week vacation and upon his return sought out the HR leader. His opening line on the call to her was "You're like a mother to me." He went on to say that he was quite disappointed to have returned from leave to find everything had gone awry. While he was gone, the COO had made the decision to move his part of the business to another city and given the team members an option to move or receive a severance package.

He felt it was a plan to move him out. He said he would have liked the opportunity to move to Charlotte, but the timing was not right for him personally. However, he disagreed with the circumstances of moving the team. He decided, therefore, it was time for him to move on, and he agreed not to go to a competitor. But he wanted to know if the company would consider hiring him as a sub-contractor, especially if a certain deal he had been working on came to fruition.

Oddly, rather than waiting for a severance package, he

chose to leave the company right away, stating it was more important to him to get on with his life. That told the HR leader that he had secured another job while out on leave. That was okay, but why wouldn't he take the extra pay?

In the end, part of the team relocated and performed well, and so the COO rewarded them. Feedback from the team was they were happy to see the porno peeper go. He was a disgruntled leader focused on the wrong thing: himself.

ADULT ACCOUNTABILITY

HR teams get beat up a lot for things that are, in fact, the employee's responsibility, and some of these things are amazing! These things include not maximizing a 401k match during the year, not remembering to add a child to the health plan, not knowing the bonus payment policy (see "Miscalculation") and not reminding people that they were maxed out on paid time off and no longer earning PTO hours. These same individuals—these *adults*—would be punishing their kids for not doing their homework or paying attention in school. Here are a few examples.

401k Match

It's early December when the benefits leader gets a call from an employee: "I've maxed out my 401k for the year, and now I'm missing out on the December match. Why didn't you tell me?" The benefits leader replies, "We send all employees a notice in the first quarter with instructions on how to maximize your 401k match and help you ensure that you take advantage of the federal maximum contribution."

The employee, who is quite irritated, responds: "You expect employees to keep track of all this with one notice months before? I'm very busy and don't have time to keep up with all the details. This is what I expect from my benefits team. This is a long-term benefit, and I will now lose several hundred dollars in my retirement account. What are you going to do about it?"

The benefits leader was quite taken aback by this rude confrontation. The leader took a deep breath and explained that it is each employee's responsibility to calculate, track, and manage their retirement plans. The company provides a plan that the employee can choose to participate in, manage their account, and make adjustments appropriate to their own personal financial goals. The benefits person was sorry that the employee missed out on some of the benefit; however, with the Employee Retirement Income Security Act (ERISA) regulations, there was nothing that could be done. He was encouraged to start planning now for next year. Needless to say, the employee was quite disgruntled at the end of the call.

I know you might find this hard to believe, but it happened again with the same employee the following year!

Oh, Baby!

Healthcare ERISA and HIPAA regulations require people to notify the company when there are significant, life-changing events. One such regulation relates to the birth or adoption of a child. An employee who has one of the events outside of the open enrollment period has thirty days to notify their employer and healthcare provider to add the child to the policy. This particular company communicated this during open enrollment, it was boldly noted on the benefits homepage, and it was included in the quarterly "lunch-n-learns." The benefits team had no way to know when employees were having babies, so they couldn't target individuals!

Although this happens sometimes, most employees, while perhaps upset about missing out, are not rude about it. But one particular salesperson did not fit into that category. The HR leader was on the way to a meeting with the benefits broker and took a call from the employee. After the niceties were exchanged, the employee went into his plea to have the HR leader make an exception. She listened and then explained that an exception could not be made. This was a matter of federal law and the company must comply with the regulations.

It was now nearly sixty days post birth, and the employee was just now bringing this up. He had received a well-baby bill that he wanted the healthcare provider or the company to pay. He was asked about his car insurance: If he got a new car, would he remember to call the insurance company? Of course he would. He didn't think it was the same situation and said that when a new baby is born, the family is quite busy! He told the HR leader that it was her team's responsibility to get this fixed! The HR leader thought, *are you kidding me?*

As far as he was concerned, he was vital to the business, and he was willing to go all the way to the CEO. The HR leader kept reiterating that the employee was responsible to take care of his family's financial and insurance needs. Unless he had told the HR team that his wife was pregnant, how was HR to know to even remind him? The leader asked him, "Did you attend open enrollment? And do you read the literature we send out?" He replied, "I didn't attend open enrollment meetings, and anything from HR goes directly to my junk file. I don't have time to read all that stuff, I'm busy with clients!"

Well there you have it. What's a benefits leader to do?

Another employee wanted to adopt a baby, and complained to benefits that she was being penalized for adopting a child since she was not entitled to the same short-term disability payments as a woman giving birth. She became quite hostile in the office towards the benefits person, so much so that employees in the vicinity left, as it was quite uncomfortable. At one point she became quite emotional and there was no calming her down. She refused to listen or understand that short-term disability is payable when you are medically and physically unable to work. There were other options for her, such as family medical leave, which while unpaid, would enable her to take up to twelve weeks of job-protected leave and she could use her paid vacation for a part of that time. The company agreed to look into potentially offering a paid parental leave plan, but it would not happen in time for her. She was very angry.

WHO NEEDS HR?

This is a rather fascinating story that was shared with me.

Not everyone believes that HR brings value, and that viewpoint is normally based on poor behavior of those individuals who don't want to change and create a respectful workplace. Of course, one person's idea of respecting others is quite different from the next person's.

A meeting was being held in a large conference room and seating was limited. A female employee entered, obviously looking for a seat. One of the male senior leaders caught her eye and slapped his lap multiple times as if suggesting that she sit on his lap. The person sitting next to the senior leader was actually heard to say, "Well, that's creepy." The female employee appeared shocked and embarrassed, and she left the room and re-entered via a different door.

The next day, the HR leader who had witnessed the behavior met with the senior leader who had made inappropriate gestures. Rather than answering for his behavior, he proceeded to berate HR and said he did not believe the organization needed an HR department, giving some examples of unsatisfactory interactions with a former member of the HR team. Later in the conversation, he retracted his statement and complimented the new HR leader on her approach to the role. He felt she was quite different from the last person.

Evidently, the guy just didn't know when to keep quiet! In that same conversation, he went on to tell the HR leader that the office was a great diverse team. "We have someone in a wheelchair!" he said. "We've got all types of people on this one team, and all we need now is a gay and a lesbian and we can tick that box!" The HR leader could not believe her ears. At the end of the meeting, he closed with: "I hope I didn't offend you or say anything wrong." He had no idea that she was considered a "triple minority"—i.e., black, gay, female—and he had just broken every possible rule! Fortunately for this company, the HR person had a high degree of tolerance and let it go for the moment. She later had a crucial conversation to "train" this senior leader and keep him from making the same mistake. That took courage!

Several months later, at another business meeting, this same senior leader, in a room of subordinates (I hate this word but what other word is there?), he started sharing some unflattering comments about the behaviors of his colleagues (CEO, SVPs, and other senior leaders) at a company sponsored event. He also gave a derogatory name to the event and disclosed how much the colleagues had been drinking, how they shouldn't have driven home, and how some sexual overtures had been made. It was very inappropriate to discuss in that setting. *No wonder he does not "need" HR,* thought the HR leader. *He doesn't "want" HR!*

On another occasion, this same person attended a meeting at a partner company. When he was introduced to a man he already knew, he said, "Of course we know each other! He's another one of those guys coming from the motherland sucking on the tits of our country!" The people who were party to this conversation excused themselves and walked away, leaving him standing there in total confusion. He stated later, "I was just having some fun!" But the question is at whose expense?

TRIPLE BREASTS

It appears that countries outside of the United States use quite liberal marketing and advertising methods known as "shock advertising." An international magazine featured an article about the CEO of this particular US company and put him on the front cover, and the company's marketing team ordered a large number of copies to share with the US workforce without reviewing the entire magazine, and copies were sent to the various offices.

Imagine the shock when people saw that on the rear cover, in living color, was a photograph of a woman with three breasts, breastfeeding her triplets! Staff was asked to rip off the rear covers and destroy them. Well, of course, not everyone complied, and it created at least one employee relations challenge that needed to be addressed.

One of the company offices had a pre-occupation with provocative behavior and chose the magazine to provoke a co-worker. An employee was sitting in his office when his co-worker came along to antagonize him. "Hey, did you know there was a photo of your wife on the back of this magazine?" he said and threw the magazine onto his colleague's desk and walked away laughing. The employee was furious! That was the last straw, and he put in a call to HR.

The antagonist thought it was a joke—he was "just having fun." He got a one-time warning and was told to apologize and leave the guy alone. He may have had a tougher consequence in today's environment. People need to keep this type of behavior outside of the workplace.

THE TEAM JERSEY CAPER

There was an off-site leadership meeting, and people from all over the world were in attendance. One of the team-building activities included a prize for the top team, but the prize (some sort of jersey that was being shipped from overseas) had not arrived. What to do? The winning team could be given an IOU with an explanation; after all, the jerseys had already been purchased!

Well, that was not good enough for the global HR leader managing the team-building exercise. She was furious! The conference chair felt she was overreacting: It's only a jersey and these were adults who will understand that things happen!

The conference chair witnessed the global so-called leader (true leaders do not do what this person did) call an employee in another country (at 9:00 p.m. the employee's time) and yell at her, demanding that she leave her house, drive to the office, and get the jerseys sent overnight for next day. The conference chair was appalled at the behavior and how this person treated that employee. After all, this company touted that "respect for the individual" was one of their values.

The global leader hung up the phone and then went on a rant in front of other staff about how that employee was inept and could not be trusted to get a simple task done. She said she would need to make a change. The conference chair and local HR leader tried to calm the leader down and explain that it would all be fine: The group would understand and they could still make the event special with capturing a photo of the jersey, printed on nice cardstock that the winners would receive in lieu of the real thing. They could get their home addresses and mail the jerseys. This seemed to calm the global leader down some, but the behavior was forever embedded in the conference chair's mind, along with the other five or six people in the room. The leader was oblivious as to how her behavior had impacted the others and how that behavior gave a negative view of the HR team overall.

It was later learned that the employee on the receiving end of the leader's tirade had had enough and resigned—all over a silly jersey! Although, it was probably the proverbial "straw that broke the camel's back," no one needs to be treated or humiliated in that way.

GET A BAND-AID

The leadership team was gathering for a joint strategy session. The meeting was being held in the hotel boardroom, and about thirteen or so people had gathered. One of the senior leaders entered the room dressed in a tight, sleeveless T-shirt, wrinkled shorts, and flip-flops. The only female in the room was shocked and appalled! The guy was not a small guy and definitely not a body-builder. That's perfectly fine, but some attire simply isn't appropriate at an executive meeting.

But it gets better! Picture this overweight guy with long underarm hair hanging out from his T-shirt, with crusty feet. He had also cut himself shaving in several places and had little pieces of toilet paper stuck to his face. The woman told him not to sit near her. Pointing to a cut on his face, she said, "That is disgusting! Get a Band-Aid for crying out loud."

Of course, you know what he did. He plopped himself right next to the female. She looked across at the CFO for help, and the CFO suggested that he leave and get himself a Band-Aid or two. He laughed all the way out of the door, while his female colleague moved his things to a place far away from her at the table.

When he returned, he moved himself right back next to her. It was going to be a very long day with this guy. He thought he was being funny, when really he was just being obnoxious and rude. Why would he do that? you might ask.

The answer is "Because he could," and no one had the guts to do anything about him.

COFFEE BREAK

This story starts out at an annual company event that has been best described as similar to the film *Animal House.*

This company used to take its employees to a small venue in the mountains for a retreat, and it was evidently a free-for-all, rowdy, anything-goes type of an event. It was fully company funded, and attendance was optional. The company actually had to put up a $10,000 bond in advance to the city to cover potential damages, this was a result of their history of damages left behind in the early years of this annual event.

Some of the leaders and their spouses/significant others who attended the event were quite chummy. One of the leaders (remember the Band-Aid guy?) was actually separated from his wife and living with one of the employees. Both the wife and the leader were fine with this arrangement, so it seemed, and they had been separated long before this particular affair started.

The venue had a hot-tub and people liked to use it; clothing was optional. On one evening, one of the other leaders and the Band-Aid guy's employee-girlfriend were having a nice soak in the buff. Someone took a photo for a keepsake.

Later that same year, the guy in the hot tub had a birthday. The employees were invited to the coffee room to celebrate, and imagine his surprise when they were all served coffee in mugs that had the hot-tub photo printed onto the cup.

A visitor from another company came in one day. He was invited to have a cup of coffee by the Band-Aid guy. He handed his visitor a coffee in the now infamous mug and waited for his reaction. The visitor was shocked and laughed nervously. The host was having a lot of fun with this and explained to his guest, that the picture was of his own girlfriend and one of the managers taken at last year's company event. "Isn't it a great culture we have here?" he said. The story goes that he said "I paid for those!" The visitor wasn't sure if he meant the cups or the quite large breasts and he wasn't going to ask for clarity on that.

The visitor went along with it but was not impressed or delighted to be drinking from that cup. This type of behavior is totally inappropriate and could be quite costly to a business in this day and age. Whether visitor or employee, no one has to be part of disrespectful behavior. There is a duty to act if a law, policy, or safety matter is involved.

BAD BOSS

This story occurred over a long period of time—more than eighteen months, in fact.

A new director was hired to improve the profit and loss of the business. The honeymoon period was great! The staff were happy, and he was upbeat, cheerful, engaged. Life was good for a short time. Sadly, it did not take long for this guy's low emotional intelligence to pop out.

The phone calls and emails started to come into HR. This guy was impulsive, and he chastised people in public; it was his way or the highway. He spent money like it was going out of fashion. It was as if he was the CEO of a large organization with lots of extra cash to throw around. He made it clear to the staff that he was the boss and that he had ultimate authority for all things in the business.

HR was asked to complete a "360 feedback" on this leader. His direct reports were contacted and asked if they would give their honest, unfiltered feedback on this report if asked. Most said yes, and looked forward to the opportunity to finally have their voices heard. Two actually called and asked if they could supplement the written feedback with a conversation, because some things were too difficult to write. (For readers not familiar with a 360 report, it is when the individuals rate themselves in different areas, their boss rates them, and several peers and direct reports also rate them. The idea is that they have the benefit of receiving feedback from everyone they work with at different levels. Except for the boss's feedback, the reports are anonymous.)

HR was told that, before their visit to the office, the director had a meeting with his staff and told them that if anyone wanted to meet with HR, they must first meet with him to ensure that they are briefed on what could be shared with HR. Failure to follow this process would mean trouble. In addition, the messages the staff got from the director were counter to the messages they got from the executive team at the company. Employees were frustrated and feeling trapped.

Some additional things learned about his behavior during the 360 process were that he was not trusted or respected. He was impulsive, unpredictable, and said one thing but did another. The team felt he oversold the clients and often appeared to be in another world, meaning that they must constantly double check reality with him. The clients and partners, apparently, did not find him credible. His favorite word about the business and the environment was "fantastic," when it was anything but! The sales folks did not want him accompanying them because he got in the way and was so boastful that he impeded the sale. One example of an embarrassing overpromise/under-deliver scenario was his promise to take a client to a global event without checking to see if there were actually tickets and space for the client. There wasn't, and he had the salesperson go back and tell the client! The salesperson wasn't even aware of the promise until he was told to let the client know he could not attend!

One area that was quite a concern to the staff was his termination of good people without consulting the managers and then replacing them with people he knew in the industry. The feeling in the office was that if this guy did not like you, it was only a matter of time before you were ousted. He regularly went around the HR process and policies, and people would simply show up to start work! This happened mostly when the HR leader would take time out of the office, and there was a lot of clean up to be done on her return.

When this guy would speak in meetings, the employees would roll their eyes. He also failed to listen and take data in; he was so busy trying to talk that nothing registered with him during the meeting, and he would have to ask for clarity later. That completely frustrated his team because most conversations had to occur twice.

People never knew whether the happy boss or mad boss was going to show up. He would talk about managers behind their backs. One-on-ones with this person always led to his colleagues wondering what he said about them to others. This led to the managers comparing notes. They discovered that one day someone was great, but the next day he or she was the worst manager or employee ever hired.

On one particular occasion, this leader told the staff at the end of the week that the numbers for the quarter looked great. Go out and have a great weekend, he told them. When they came in on Monday, he called them all in and let them know that things were bleak. They had a six-figure loss, and there was no way they would be able to overcome that loss in a short time. That was almost the last straw for many; they could not trust this guy. He had no credibility with his direct reports or even his boss!

The leaders got together and formed a plan to elevate the issue to senior leadership. His "soft skills" were so lacking that he could not continue as their leader. He needed to go. They were tired of the outright lies, the cattiness and boasting, the hiring of friends and firing of perfectly good employees, and the commissioning of expensive art work (they were losing money, yet he commissioned over $20,000 of art work for the office!). He was spoiling their reputation in the market, and his unethical behavior was embarrassing. The team was done with him!

They wanted to know what it was going to take to move this guy out. Well, as with most people like this, it was only a matter of time before he really sunk himself. He made a huge commitment that a deal was to come in. He stated that the company was one of the top two on the short list and he had "an in" with the decision maker. Well, he did not have the "in" and, of course, there was no deal! That was basically the final nail. Change in leadership needed to happen.

As the story goes, the conversation with him was rather interesting. He was shocked and felt like he had been wrongly accused of poor leadership. He had an excuse or reason for each problem cited and took accountability for none of the business failures or challenges.

This is a good example of following your gut sooner rather than later. It was not too long after this person was put in place that things started to go awry. More than eighteen months later, the business was looking for a new leader, a process that could have been started twelve months earlier. Sometimes you do need to give people chances, but sometimes you need to move quickly to reduce your losses and save your employees from pure hell.

There are many more stories starring this guy, but you get the picture!

GIGGLES AND JIGGLES

Sometimes, guys just can't help themselves. This story dates back a few years, but the author knows that there are many people who still hold some of the beliefs this person had about what was okay to share at work. It wasn't okay then, and it still isn't okay, especially from a leader to an employee!

After attending a leadership development program, a call was made to the HR leader's office. One of the attendees of the program wanted to share that she did not speak up a lot in the training sessions because she was quite uncomfortable. She explained that one of the male leaders, who used to be her boss, would know that if she spoke up with examples about workplace issues she would be referencing *his* behavior. She was concerned about retaliation for exposing him.

When this guy first became her manager, he shared with her that he had been "reported to HR" by a female salesperson he referred to as the "Mafia Princess." He shared that she was just a "sissy" for reporting him. He further stated that she got whatever she wanted and thought she could push people around, "getting her boys on it" if she didn't get her way (see Rat Poison Takes Care of Rats story). He shared that there had been others that reported him to HR, but he saw no value in HR and wished that the United States was more like his home country, South Africa, where there seemed to be no use for HR.

It was not uncommon for him to bring up abortion and religion in negative ways. He did this always in a mixed group and pontificated his point of view on the topics, either seeking a reaction or an affirmation that he was correct in his beliefs.

During the 2008 US Presidential election, he spoke up about the issue of gay marriage, which was in the headlines and a big part of the presidential campaign (it remains a hot topic to this day!). His exact words were "I don't agree with it. They should not be able to get married. Marriage is between a man and a woman. I know your brother is gay, I can see you are getting uncomfortable right now, but I really feel this way." The complainant felt powerless to say anything about his comments, again fearful she would be retaliated against, maybe not openly but subtly. He was her manager and as such had control of her career.

This employee did not come forward for several years and had lived with this resentment far too long. Fortunately for her, he moved to another state in the interim and those in her office who had to deal with him were apparently thrilled that he was no longer around. She was reminded of his behavior and overbearing comments when she found herself in the leadership development program with this guy. All the history of his unfiltered words came back. She was disappointed that she felt she could not fully engage in the program with him present.

She shared that the very first time she met him, they were reviewing a document for a client and he said to her "This is the first time I've ever seen you as more than giggles and jiggles!" She was flabbergasted. She provided the names of a few female colleagues in his new office location who were now experiencing his unprofessional and derogatory innuendos.

The last thing she shared was that he stopped by the HR office one day and saw two women talking to each other. He told one of them, a manager, that she would make a perfect fill-in for the front desk because she was a female with a fantastic smile. She responded by walking out of the office, commenting: "I cannot believe you just said that, and in the HR office too!" From what the employee reported, this was normal behavior in the office for this guy, and the local HR person did nothing to coach or guide him. That company was very lucky that no one filed what could have been a very costly complaint. To her knowledge, he was never reprimanded for his behavior.

HR missed an opportunity to coach and potentially change his behavior by not addressing this early on. The HR person left the organization exposed to future unprofessional and illegal behavior in the workplace. His statements contributed to a hostile work environment.

PRACTICAL JOKES ... SORT OF

These are just some short, funny quips I have been given over the years.

A sales leader and CEO were good friends. The sales leader was aware that a partner in sales had a "crush" on the CEO, so he set up a lunch meeting between them. When the CEO arrived, it quickly became apparent that he had been set up on a date with a gay man. He finished the lunch and came back to the office confronting his sales leader, laughing, "Okay, that one will be hard to top. Watch your back!"

When a male manager was performance managing a young, attractive female, she complained to HR that he was spending more time "looking her up and down" than he was training her. When asked about it by HR, his response was that it was the funniest thing I've ever heard. He had to be made to realize that this was not a joke.

At a team-building event at a ski resort during the off-season, a leader asked someone to tell a funny joke. A guy stands up and tells an offensive joke aimed at a certain religion. Most of the room was insulted, and the room was filled with a hushed silence. So much for team building—after that, the group was separated!

———————

A new HR manager received a sexual harassment complaint by a male accusing women of harassing him during the night shift. This got out and became a company joke with men commenting "Oh, I wish they'd harass me." No one believed him, and he became ostracized. But a video camera caught the women taking off their tops and hitting him with their breasts! They surrounded him and teased him. Once he reported the incidents, they filed a counter-complaint alleging he was harassing them. They demanded to be moved to the day shift and to be paid the night shift rate to get away from him. When the HR person shared the video with them, they started crying and turned on each other, one blaming the other for instigating the harassment against this man. The resolution took so long that he finally resigned and sued because he was continuously harassed throughout the investigation. He should have been given leave with pay until the investigation was completed. Poor HR work.

———————

Two guys were attending a conference together. They'd worked together for a while. One called the other a "brother Dutchman." Well, if you don't know much about slang in South Africa, this is actually a derogatory term for a white Afrikaner. The offended employee let the guy know that this was a derogatory comment, explained why, and they moved on.

Fast forward five years and the guy said it again, this

time to a CIO of another company and in front of the same guy he had insulted before, who was livid! The crazy thing is that this guy's manager was there when he said it five years before, made excuses for him, saying, "I'm sure he forgot what happened five years ago. The guy is just stupid sometimes!"

Given that this guy had presented numerous challenges to the business over the years, the boss was asked if "the juice was worth the squeeze." The boss definitely thought the guy was "good juice" and promised to keep working with the guy to keep his head straight.

My former colleague wrote this about the photo below: "I staged this picture to pair up the inappropriate T-shirt with our always appropriate HR leader. She didn't know it until many years later, but I've always had this picture assigned to her contact in my iPhone!"

Sometimes friends just can't be trusted!

FACEBOOK MATTERS

One of the sales folks at a company, in the early days of the Black Lives Matter movement posted this on Facebook:

"Black lives don't matter. If you are a dumb ass with a record a mile long (black or white), are doing something illegal or have just done something illegal like you being a belligerent dumb ass to the police. You get what's coming. Society is better off without you."

He was appropriately reprimanded and immediately took down the comment. He said he just got so frustrated with all the riots and violence that he spouted off without thinking. Isn't that how most verbal conflict occurs-reacting rather than thinking before responding?

You may be exercising your freedom of speech or citing the United States Constitution. However, as an employee, you have the duty to represent the company professionally. As a person in sales, who indicates in your Facebook profile the company you work for, you must be careful what you post as it impacts your personal brand and the company's brand. Clients, partners, or fellow employees reading such a post would surely be offended and would not want to do business with or work alongside you. There are just some statements that you do not post to the public, especially if you are a commissioned salesperson! Just sayin'...

FLIGHT ATTENDANT FRENZY

People often think that those who have travel jobs really have it made. They get to see the world, be away from reality, and life is grand! Well, after one particularly tough travel week, one person had the following story to tell.

She departed Raleigh, NC to meet up with her boyfriend in Chicago for the weekend, but she had to rearrange her schedule and that made for a tight connection. It took some time to get everyone seated, and the flight was beginning to look delayed. She walked to the front of the plane and started chatting with the flight attendant to seek advice. While she was talking, in mid-sentence, the flight attendant turned and went into the front bathroom! She then started chatting with the other flight attendant before getting back to her seat. Neither had offered any real assistance, but at least the second one wasn't rude.

The flight took off, and drinks were served. Mid-flight, the employee got up and went to the rear of the aircraft to talk with a third flight attendant. The first flight attendant who had rudely turned away from her, arrived in the rear of the aircraft to get something. The employee looked at the flight attendant and commented that she didn't appreciate the earlier rudeness. The flight attendant actually put up her hand in the employee's face as if to say, "I don't want to hear it" and walked away again! The employee then told the rear

flight attendant that she was going to post the photo of that flight attendant on the airline's Facebook page.

During the ensuing weekend, she did as she promised and posted a photo she had taken of the rude flight attendant, along with a caption directed to customer service at the airline that described her experience after a long and difficult work week. She further stated that she had been a long-time customer of this airline and this was the first and only bad experience. She ended with inviting them to contact her if they were interested in chatting about the experience.

Never did she anticipate the fury by the airline employees that ensued from that posting on Facebook! There were over a hundred comments about their outrage with the customer posting a photo of one of their own. The woman said she just read the comments and didn't defend her post; all she wanted was for the flight attendant to be reprimanded and given guidance on a better way to deal with passengers.

What she learned, however, is that it is illegal to post photos of flight attendants on a social site without their permission! There is supposedly some FAA regulation about it (I did not check this but took the contributor at their word). She could not believe the fallout from her action. It was never her intention to break a law; she simply wanted her complaint to be heard. Who would have thought?

SEXUAL INNUENDOS

The following snippets are indicative of the crazy things that people say in a business environment that create challenges for HR folks because most are borderline illegal or just plain inappropriate!

1. Overheard in New York by a male salesperson to a much younger female colleague: "Your bra's too tight!" This guy had daughters her age, and probably thought he was parenting his daughter! He thought it was funny; she thought he was a creepy old man. Of course, HR had to intervene.

2. A senior leader introduced an employee to an external vendor: "You don't have to remember her name because she is leaving to go fuck men for a year." Needless to say, the vendor was shocked, and the employee was beet red. Neither said a word in response. Why wouldn't you speak up?

3. Waiting for a meeting to start, a leader started a discussion regarding bestiality. Who would bring up such a topic anywhere much less in an office setting?

4. A new, acting senior leader was in a meeting and dropped the F-bomb at least six times. No one spoke up. Fear stifles people. What has happened to respect for others, especially given that respect for the individual and integrity were two of this company's core values?

5. Leadership call:

John says, "I've got no pants on."

Laughter.

John says, "I'm sitting in Bob's chair."

Louder laughter.

Bob then says: "Okay, John, just don't tell me you had Mexican for lunch!"

Roaring laughter by all except the women on the call.

6. Two guys were talking with a female sales rep:

First guy: "Have you had anal sex with your husband?"

Second guy: "That's the only way to have sex with her."

First guy: "Are you a fucking idiot to talk that way in front of her?"

Word got back to leadership, and it was noted that the first guy was a powder keg in front of women. The woman merely stated that "in this industry, women take it on the chin." However, there was always a concern that if she needed to go on a performance improvement plan, it could be problematic given the inappropriate work environment.

7. One sales leader had no idea how to speak with professional women. Here are a few of his comments:

Is it your time of the month? Is *that* your problem?

Don't go hormonal on me!

I'm using my 3:00 a.m. voice, sweetie.

8. At a leadership forum event, in front of peers, one leader confronted another leader on a situation and shouted at him "you stupid, big, fat idiot." The recipient was mortified.

These are all prime examples of the lack of leadership, the lack of emotional intelligence and the company doing nothing to create a workplace free of hostile behavior. If the reader finds themselves in situations like these, speak up or get out! When someone has been blatantly belittled and embarrassed in front of peers, people need to speak up and stop the behavior—while it can be risky, it's worth it. Retaliation is against the law.

Each of these situations contributes could create a hostile work environment, could cost people their jobs, could cost the company millions and, the author is confident, they go against the behavior policies of these organizations. When you read the headlines today, it's still amazing that people cannot believe that these things happen in business. It happens every day all around the world. It's also amazing that professionals, both male and female, condone this talk and behavior. Everyone has a responsibility to protect the company's name, image, and assets, but for whatever reason, people are failing miserably to speak up. It's even more fascinating as many of these people have children! What kind of future work environment do they want to create for the future? The same advice given regarding criminal behavior should apply to poor behavior in the workplace: If you see something, say something.

LEADERSHIP BULLYING

The following comments were made to an HR generalist by an employee about the bullying behavior of his manager.

'You don't get on the wrong side of her or you will get the short end of the stick.'

'She has done many unprofessional things over the years, and if I had been her boss I would have done something about it.'

'She's wanted me out of the business for quite some time, and I don't even report to her.'

'My boss disclosed to me that he has had consistent challenges with managing things with her. She wants things done her way, even if it is not the correct way.'

'If she doesn't get what she wants, she uses bullying, intimidation, and fear as a means to manage. She has done that for years.'

'She made sure that, since I didn't help her, I didn't get to go on trip.'

'I was invited to a partner event, which was okayed by my manager, she found out I went and made a big stink about it, using vile and foul language to my manager. Incredible she was not reprimanded for that!'

'She has undermined me since I began. On one particular RFP (request for proposal), my manager specifically gave direction that no one was to work on it because it was a losing proposal for the company. Upset by this decision, she came into the office and yelled at the entire team in front of the rest of the office and even commented loudly, "Your organization sucks."'

'She puts on a great show and persona of teamwork and collaboration, but her attitude is *I'm right; you're wrong*. She has been yelling at her sales teams for years and nothing is done.'

'She does not know the meaning of "team." She's a teller, not a doer, and people are afraid of her.'

WOW! Just the kind of leader that I would want to work with or for! She could use a page out of the listening book about responding vs. reacting. (What's the difference you might ask? Responding is a thoughtful response with emotions intact, while reacting is an impulsive, with high emotions and tends to shut down the other person). "Listen more, talk less" would also be helpful. How about the old adage of do unto others? Or what about simple respect? Not to be preachy, but if this sounds like any manager or leader you know, get out from under them while you can!

THE GREAT AND POWERFUL OZ

There is an assumption in organizations that the executive team has it easy: they make all the decisions, they make the big bucks, they travel, and the list goes on. That may be true in some organizations, but certainly not all. Here's an interesting story for the reader to contemplate. How would you feel if this happened to you?

Once upon time, at a company in Kansas, there was an executive team that had been in place for a few years. One day, the CEO resigned to spend more time with his family. Then, about two weeks later, the CFO also resigned without stating any reason.

The top guy of the global company came to visit the remaining team to discuss what should be done. Two important roles needed to be filled and the business needed to be held together. He sought the counsel of the team and a decision was made to fill the CEO role from within the organization (there was a lot of support for the naming of this person to the CEO role) and to seek external candidates for the CFO role. In addition, he wanted to keep the rest of the leadership team in place, so he put together an Executive Employment Agreement to entice them to stay and grow the business. All signed the agreement. They stayed and the business and the team prospered.

About ten years later, enter a new global leader. A decision was made that the company should attempt to renegotiate the employment agreements for "standardization" reasons. By this time, several of the original signors of the Executive Employment Agreement had departed and there were only a few team members left with these agreements. Conversations ensued, the holders did not want a "new deal"; they were quite happy with the one they had.

Pressure was applied from "Oz," the great and powerful global leader. If they didn't agree, the company would withhold equity, and no future equity will be granted to them. Oz wanted performance without compensation! This company had stated values of accountability and respect for the individual. It always talked about their great people, won awards for the workplace environment, and talked about a winning culture. It did not seem those things mattered when Oz was dealing with the leadership team that was expected to deliver on the promises to clients.

The problem was that the new agreements took away certain rights that existed in the original contract, and there was no consideration (a legal term) to compensate for the change. The new agreements were one-sided to the company. After the many years of blood, sweat, and tears to keep the company moving forward, this was the thanks being given! The interesting thing about this was that the company was the original drafter of the agreement in the beginning; it was the company's deal and now they wanted to change it.

The new deal was a take-it or leave-it deal. It wasn't up for debate and the choice was either sign and get equity but lose certain very important clauses, or don't sign and lose equity but get the very important protections that would have been eliminated. What a way to lead from the front! Remember

that line from the *Wizard of Oz* ? "The Great and Powerful Oz has spoken. Now go!"

The executives said "no deal" but they didn't want to go. They liked their job and the people they worked with and they were making a difference every day.

During the last conversation, Oz specifically stated there was "no risk of any of you losing your job in the future." Would you be surprised that six months later, one of the executive's roles was eliminated? Had he signed the "new deal" his departure would have been much less lucrative than it was with the original deal. Now there were three left with the original deal. Before the year was up, another resigned—why stay without equity and with a leadership that bullies their executives to give up rights granted by the company? Five weeks later, two more executives were forced out, leaving one. Not four months later the final executive was gone. Oz got his wish. Wouldn't it just have been simpler to move them out all at once and rip off the Band-Aid, so to speak?

But wait! There's another story about the Great and Powerful Oz. A few years before the agreement debacle, executives were required to pay back a bonus that was earned according to the compensation policy. Only the executives were forced to pay back the bonus; the employee population kept their bonuses that year. That's another story of some of the shenanigans you can pull if you are the Great and Powerful Oz! Oz then changed the policy document to keep that from happening again, another policy that the company drafted in the first place!

FINANCIAL SOAP OPERA

A new finance leader was hired at a company and she was soon enjoying her new-found power. She seemed to enjoy making demands, stomping around the office, and simply intimidating others. Here are a few examples.

A recruiter and HR generalist were reviewing potential new hires and job offers. The walls were thin, so they were working behind closed doors. The finance leader opened the door and demanded to know why they were working in private. They didn't even report to this person.

Another person was working on payroll and needed quiet. Her instant message notification kept popping up demanding that she come to the finance leader's office. Every sixty seconds, she was getting pinged. She didn't really have a chance to respond, it was crazy! Of course, whatever it was that she was needed for was not urgent or life threatening; it was simply intimidation.

A contractor was sitting at her desk working. The finance leader walked in and demanded that she move her things to allow for someone else to take that spot. She was demanding it in front of everyone. If she did not move immediately, she would have someone come in and move her!

Everything with this person was urgent, and whatever you were working on was not important. She was rude and disrespectful. Her team had gone to HR seeking advice because they are afraid to talk with her. She was not approachable, and they did not want to get on her bad side (although they said they didn't think she had a good side!). She was harsh with her comments, did not accept ideas from others, and her behavior indicated that her Emotional Quotient (EQ) was low.

The senior leaders in this organization were oblivious to this leader's shortcomings and were not open to hearing examples of poor behavior. In fact, she won a very prestigious leadership award, which shut down all conversation with the staff. They saw the situation as hopeless, and that then led to high turnover.

I am sure that there are many readers that can relate to this unfortunate scenario in their careers. The only option is to move on quickly!

#BULLYBOSSLADY

Sometimes, guys get a bad rap for being a bully in the workplace, but it's not always the men who are bullies! This story is about a Southern Belle who was a Doctor Jekyll and Mrs. Hyde.

She was considered a strong leader who ran a tight ship. What no one realized was just how strictly the team was run and how bad the conditions were for employees who were subjected to them day in and day out over a period of years.

People were so afraid of her that they wouldn't even report the poor working conditions! It was quite disheartening when it all came to light because one of the cherished values of this company was "respect for the individual."

Once someone finally got up the courage to say something, it was very eye opening. To anyone not on her team, she was polite, friendly, funny, engaging—the epitome of Southern charm. The senior leaders praised her quite often, and she had been rewarded with recognition and inclusion in leadership special events. Overall, she was well thought of as a future senior leader.

The HR person conducted a team inquiry to learn more about the "team culture," as it appeared to not be aligned with the company culture. It was determined that this leader had a 58 percent "approval" rating. "Subtle bullying" was the term often used. She clearly had favorites on the team with whom she went to lunch most days of the week, and some team members were never invited. The tone of her voice and her mannerisms were described as negative and condescending. Not everyone was held to the same rules.

It was perceived that she was always "digging for dirt" on those she did not favor, and it depended on where you were in her favoritism spectrum as to how lenient her managing style was. There was one person she hated in particular, and if a team member got along with this person, it was obvious that he or she soon fell out of favor with the #bullybosslady. The perception was that she was insincere, and people wondered who else she was talking about and gathering dirt on? The fear of retaliation ran rampant on this team, and she promoted only those in her favor, regardless of performance.

All of this was brought to the attention of her leader, who was quite hesitant to take any action. It was believed that the complaints were coming from a few "low performers" who had it in for their boss. He did not see her as #bullybosslady. No way could this be true!

HR knew it was only a matter of time before this would come to a head. And it did. A few months later, a letter from the Equal Employment Opportunity Commission arrived (EEOC). The allegation was discrimination under the Americans Disability Act (ADA). The allegation had been made by an employee who had been let go suddenly. Apparently, she had let #bullybosslady know that she was going to be taking maternity leave in the coming months, and the very next day she was discharged for poor performance ... sacked before anyone even knew that she was with child! Evidently, #bullybosslady had not given her a verbal warning or a written performance warning before letting her go.

As with all of these types of cases, there is mandatory

mediation. During the preparation for the mediation, a lot of allegations emerged about what it was really like to work for #bullybosslady. The company chose to get through the mediation and settle the case. Subsequently, #bullybosslady was also discharged for poor leadership performance.

RAT POISON TAKES CARE OF RATS

This is a very interesting case that involved a salesperson who was quite the character and had "creative" ways of doing business for her employer. This person was quite secretive and operated under the radar, and she was seemingly above reproach because she brought the deals in. However, this company was clear that all deals were to be done with high integrity and accountability.

The company had a contract with a large government organization and had received a lot of public recognition for this project. However, underlying this project was a lot of drama with the team, and the business imploded once the lies and deceit were uncovered. The salesperson designated herself a "leader" without authority or consent by the company, and she controlled all communications in and out of the team. She kept the status of sales close to her vest.

Some of the things she did included hiring a family member onto the team without disclosing the relationship; hiring the significant other of the family member without disclosing that relationship; offering another employee a promotion to join the team with a six-figure salary without the authority to do so; trying to hire a family member of a client without authority to "help the decision-maker out"; and making threatening statements to members of her team to "keep them in line" such as, "It will only take a shovel and some lime to take care of this."

One of her team members reported that she referred to him in emails as either "Junior," "Little Shit," "Smart Ass," or "Kid" as a way of demeaning and intimidating him as a professional in the workplace, especially since the emails go to the entire team.

An email was uncovered that showed the level of secrecy she tried to instill in the team, which stated: "Keep the conversation we had last night about hiring XXX between 'us girls.' I will explain in detail when you get back to the office." She defended her actions by trying to explain that if she let her manager know what was going on with her clients, others would try to step in and take the business away from her. She really did not get the idea that she did not own the clients! The clients contracted with the company, not with her personally. Nevertheless, when this all came to light, she kept insisting that "I just run my own thing."

Throughout the course of the HR and legal inquiry, this person could not believe how much time and energy the company was spending digging into "her business." She figured out that several people had come forward with complaints about how she was operating. That definitely did not sit well with her, and she started making her own inquiries. One such inquiry started out with a blatant statement to a member of her team: "Three people have made accusations about me. If you are going to complain, you need to clean out your own backyard first. I'm not directing this at you, I'm just putting it out there for people to think about. You know, we use rat poison to take care of rats!" The employee was quite taken aback by this and other comments designed to intimidate her and others on the team.

It seemed this "leader" would morph her behavior to

match the people she was dealing with, based on her perception of what they could tolerate. She preyed on the weak, and
one of her tactics was to say things loudly enough to touch
the buttons of those in the vicinity of her voice. She had a
great ability to make people around her feel uncomfortable.
She and one of the team members seemed to work best by
yelling at each other, no matter who was around. It was quite
the volatile work environment. Of course, the yelling did not
occur when any of the business leaders were in the office.

Another employee reported that she made a very loud
comment after another report of intimidation: "We should
put a bullet in his head! That motherfucker—look what he did
to us!" The employee said the woman was not able to focus
on the business issue; she was too focused on the person
and the anger she was feeling for being "betrayed." That
appeared to be her normal mode of operating—it was always
personal for her, never about the business.

This woman believed that the HR person she had been
interviewed by was the most unprofessional person she
had ever met. The HR person recounted the meeting a little
differently. She stated that the person in question walked into
her office, closed the door, and said she was just there to say
hello. She stood over the HR person who was sitting at her
desk, doing her best to try to intimidate her. The HR person
was calm and direct and laid it on the line, relaying what she
had been hearing from people in the office, especially the
intimidation. The employee denied that she had failed to
disclose the family connections of recent hires. She continued by adding that she had little use for her "manager" to
whom she referred to as the "NFG" (New Fucking Guy). How
many people would say that to the HR person investigating
their behavior?

Later that same day, she was speaking loudly enough on the phone for others to hear that "XX could not be trusted. Another sales person had built the account and XX came along and stole the account." Throwing yet another colleague under the bus in a way to intimidate anyone within earshot. It was apparent that she was intelligent, tactical, and calculating in her business dealings. It was felt that she was on a mission to discredit anyone who she believed had betrayed her or was seen as a threat to her operation.

All of this occurred when there was a focus in the media on bullying in the workplace. It was reported that she seemed to be purposely applying the bullying tactics she read about to her everyday dealings with people in the office. At the end of the day, as there was a very large deal on the table waiting to be awarded, the company decided to keep her, but on a very short leash, until the decision on the deal was made by the client. After that, it would be time to move her out and move on. A risky decision based on her demeanor in the office, she could explode at any time, having already created a hostile work environment and legal exposure.

It was made very clear to this individual that she was receiving a one-time warning. She was told the walls of secrecy were coming down and there would be no more intimidation; she would no longer be free to "run her own business" without keeping her manager informed. She was to play by the company rules not the other way around. The company was very confident that she would not be able to abide by this for long, but they also knew she wanted the commission once the deal closed, so she'd keep her nose clean long enough for that to happen.

Well, everyone thought that was the end of the story.

However, it was later discovered that even after this person departed the company, she just couldn't help herself. First, she tried filing a law suit alleging failure to pay commission. Failing that, she resorted to a suit alleging retaliation. Neither case went anywhere because the company called her bluff!

Several years later, this woman was implicated in a criminal case of forgery, and the following story about her was pulled from the newspaper and shared with HR:

SALES REP.'S 'FORGE SCAM'

A sales representative for a software firm admitted to forging the name of a city official on a $8.5 million government contract in an attempt to land a six-figure commission, authorities reported yesterday.

The Department of Investigation charged that XXX, an account executive at XXX Software, submitted a licensing agreement supposedly signed by a deputy commissioner at the Department of Information Technology and Telecommunications. But the autograph was actually a computerized cut-and-paste job.

She told authorities that she acted at the behest of her supervisor, XXX, who was as anxious as she was to get the deal done by the March 31 deadline so they and other executives could qualify for huge end-of-the-quarter bonuses.

But she claimed she never instructed anyone to fabricate a signature.

"In my gut, I knew it wasn't right," she told DOI.

The case was referred to the XXX DA for possible criminal charges.

BELITTLING REMARKS

A young woman in sales was asked to participate on a video call with a particular client for training purposes. Afterwards, she called the salesperson on the account and thanked him for allowing her to be on the call even though she did not contribute to the conversation. He replied, "Oh no, you added the looks!" She was not happy with that comment and let it be known to her boss.

At another dinner a comment was made by one of her colleagues: "An attractive woman like you married to a lawyer, why do you need to work?" Her male counterparts were increasingly frustrating her with these belittling comments. Her boss said he'd like to get out in front of this before it became a real problem, but he actually did nothing.

Six months later he presented her with a performance plan. She let it be known that most of the challenges she was having had to do with contending with the old-boys' club. One of the guys kept handing her trash and telling her that it was her job to get rid of trash because he thought it was funny. They wouldn't allow her into their accounts, even though it was her job to support the account, as they believed they owned the accounts.

She let the HR generalist know that her mother was the HR leader in a Fortune 500 company and her husband was an attorney, and she was seeking their advice. This spooked the generalist, and he felt obliged to continue having conversations with her, as he didn't want to say/do the wrong thing, especially since she had advised HR she was pregnant! She started to have some health issues with her pregnancy and decided to leave the organization, but not before letting it be known that, in her view, a woman could not be successful working with this group of guys. One actually apologized to her for their boorish behavior as she was departing.

HR and legal were glad to dodge a bullet. However, the leadership team in that area still did nothing to address the risk that this group of guys created.

AIN'T MISBEHAVIN'

This is a story of a female who was overpowered by males in sales roles.

She was not happy with her sales compensation plan and refused to sign it. A month later, the two sales leaders decided they needed to move this person out of the business. They alleged that she was combative, her sales performance was low, she pushed people to their limits, and she brought nothing to the table but issues (for which she offered no solutions).

There was a dinner meeting between the woman and the sales leaders. While this started as a performance review, after dinner the tone changed, and a suggestion was made to offer this person a severance package.

However, it appeared that one or more of the guys in attendance at the dinner had been inappropriate with her. They told HR that if the company tried to terminate her, it could be problematic. HR was concerned: What happened at the dinner?!

Feedback was that there was very poor language during the dinner, the waitress was being inappropriately touched by employees, and she actually asked to be relieved from serving the table! Of course, when additional questions were asked about this, there was total denial, and one person even indicated he was so drunk that he had no idea what went on that night! They further stated that the female employee appeared quite angry and threatened to sue for at least two reasons: failure to pay her commissions correctly and an unprofessional, hostile work environment.

When questioned again, the sales leaders stated, "It was no more than locker room banter at dinner." The senior guy said he asked the team later to "clean up their conversations in the presence of female employees." The decision was made to terminate the employment relationship with this female and ensure that she was paid all commissions due in exchange for a full release. The actual conversation with her is said to have gone quite well; she simply wanted to be made whole and was happy to move on. No suit was ever filed. That company was lucky it got away with inappropriate behavior that created a hostile business environment.

RECONSTRUCTION CAPER

Not all countries have the same insurance processes as the United States, and this is a story told to me by a colleague in another country.

The HR leader received an email from the insurance carrier reflecting a direct pay for an employee's hysterectomy and muscle restraint procedure. The following day, the carrier wrote to the physician seeking more information and a "medical study" and copied HR on the request. On the third day, the carrier came back and said they would require a second opinion because the documentation now reflected a hysterectomy and reconstruction of the abdomen.

The person that could approve or consent to the second opinion was away on vacation (in that country, the named insured person must consent). The carrier stated that if there was no second opinion, they would decline to cover the claim. The HR leader contacted the employee so as not to have the surgery delayed.

The employee decided to play hardball (it was his wife) and told the insurance company that if they wanted a second opinion, they could come to the hospital before the scheduled surgery and get it. The surgery was to take place at noon, and she could be seen at 8:00 a.m. for the second opinion. Now, you know that would not fly in the United States!

The insurance carrier called the patient and learned that

part of the surgery was a cosmetic procedure she had elected to have done at the same time. She had the surgery and the bill was submitted for four separate surgeries! She had a hysterectomy, a hernia surgery, a tummy tuck, and liposuction. To further complicate the matter and increase cost, she elected to use a physician that was out of network.

When the insurance company reviewed the case, after all expenses were submitted, they paid 100 percent of the hysterectomy, 100 percent for the hernia, 50 percent of the hospital stay and nothing else. Elective cosmetic surgery is not a covered expense.

Why is this a story? Well the insured person is a decision-maker in the business and has power over which carrier will get the business. The waters became quite muddy when threats to not renew the contract emerged, and it became an ethical dilemma for the HR leader who also reported to him.

The challenge was elevated and resolved appropriately but not without a sour taste in some people's mouths over the handling of this. Leaders are not to ask for decisions to be made against policy for their own personal benefit while forcing the workforce to abide strictly by the written policy. Quite a tricky situation for the HR team when this comes up.

DRINK & DEBAUCHERY

THE IM CAPER

Sue: I want him to leave me alone!

HR specialist: What's going on?

Sue: Ted's bothering me. He's making advances, and I just want to come to work and do my job.

HR specialist: Before we go any further, have you in any way encouraged him?

Sue: No! He just won't leave me alone, no matter what I do. He IMs me constantly, and I cannot get my work done. It's hard to focus.

HR specialist: Okay. The first thing I'll do is get IT to give me access to your and his IM history. I'm asking you again, will I see anything in the IM history that will show you participated with his advances?

Sue: I deleted my IMs.

HR specialist: You need to know that everything is backed up on our servers, so nothing is ever completely deleted.

Sue: I just want him to leave me alone.

HR specialist: Thanks for coming to me. I'll chat with him today and get back to you.

(The HR specialist called her boss for direction on what to do. She was advised to contact IT and ask for a download of IM history for the past ninety days for both employees.

Once that had been ordered, she was to chat with Ted and get his story. IT said they would have the info to her in twenty-four hours.)

HR specialist: Thanks for coming in, Ted. I need to talk with you about a complaint I've received from Sue regarding your interfering with her work. Can you describe your relationship with Sue for me?

Ted (looking shocked): Sue has never said that I was interfering with her work! We message back and forth throughout the day. I thought she liked me! Why didn't she just tell me rather than coming to HR?

HR specialist: Are your IMs work related or personal?

Ted: We have been flirting on IM for a while now. I'd share with you, but I delete my IMs daily.

HR specialist: Well, we store the history of IMs on our servers, and I've asked IT to provide me the last ninety days of messages for both of you. What will I find?

Ted: I don't think there's anything to be found except some work info and casual conversations between friends.

HR specialist: Great! I need you to go back to work and to cease messaging her. This is very serious. Once I review the IM history I'll have another chat with you both to hopefully close this. I ask that you not have any conversations with her until you and I chat again. This conversation is confidential and not to be discussed with anyone. Thanks for your time.

(The HR specialist received the IM history before the day ended and was shocked by what she read. Halfway through, she called her manager.)

HR specialist: You are not going to believe this IM history!

Head of HR: Nothing surprises me anymore. What's the gist?

HR specialist: I had to stop reading. It reads like a steamy novel. The sexual innuendos are blatant, the amount of time they are messaging when they're supposed to be working is ridiculous!

Head of HR: Both are actively participating in the banter?

HR specialist: Absolutely! Sometimes he starts the messaging and sometimes she starts. She is married and even talks about her relationship with her husband and how he doesn't talk to her the way that Ted talks to her. She told him she is flattered and that he makes her feel beautiful with his words. It goes sideways from there and some of the comments I'm too embarrassed to read, much less share with you. It seems that this has been progressing over time and he has gotten bolder with contacting her via cell when she's off work. It seems her husband has noticed she is "different" and she has recently realized the situation she's in and she wants out! She's scared. But it appears that Ted does not want this to end. I think we should terminate both of them. This is totally inappropriate behavior during work hours and on our equipment and systems!

Head of HR: It looks like we have both policy and values violations by both. Send me the IM history; I'll review and advise tomorrow.

That night, the head of HR sat in bed reading the IM log.

She couldn't believe what she was reading. It was right out of a steamy novel—only this was not a novel; it was happening right in her workplace! At one point, Ted was in his car in the parking lot and invited Sue to look out the office window to watch him "take care of himself," an experience about which they both then messaged later in the day! *Good grief*, she thought, *You really cannot make this shit up.*

The next day, the head of HR called the HR specialist and concurred that both parties needed to go. They had violated too many policies and were definitely not living the company's values of integrity, respect, and accountability.

The HR specialist then met with both Ted and Sue's managers to let them know what was going on. Both were shocked and appalled and agreed 100 percent that the pair needed to be removed from the business. They said they would sit in on the conversations. Ted was first. His manager was more nervous and apprehensive than Ted. As the manager began stumbling over his words, the HR specialist took over the discussion.

HR specialist: This discussion is to follow-up our conversation yesterday when you stated you had done nothing wrong. I received the IM log late yesterday, and there are numerous violations of policy and values in the conversations between you and Sue over the past few months. There are long periods of time when you are messaging each other when we were paying you to do work, not to have flirtatious conversations. You are welcome to review the logs or we can agree that this is what was found.

Ted: I don't know what to say. I liked her, I thought she liked me. She never once asked me to leave her alone. She liked my compliments. I'm sorry if she misunderstood.

HR specialist: Ted, this is serious. The things I read in the IM log are X-rated, and you wasted hours of company time. Your behavior and actions were against policy and against our values, which you are well aware exist in our business. For these reasons, your employment is terminated effective immediately.

Ted: You have to be kidding me! I was simply trying to be friends with a coworker. She never told me that my interest in her was not wanted.

HR specialist: Ted, this is not up for debate. I hope that you take the lessons from this experience and that you change your behavior in the workplace in your next place of employment. Let's go over your exit information.

After the HR specialist excused Ted's manager, she completed the paperwork and sent Ted on his way. While he was not happy (who would be if they are fired?), she was sure he knew deep down that he had been in the wrong.

Now it was time to chat with Sue. The HR specialist did a "rinse and repeat" by getting Sue's manager in the office before calling Sue in. This conversation went a little differently, in that Sue's manager wanted to handle the conversation. Here's how it went:

Sue's manager: Sue, I've asked HR to join me in this conversation. HR has advised me that you came in asking for Ted to leave you alone. You advised that while you had received messages from Ted, you had not participated in the conversations and that you simply wanted him to stop. When asked whether or not you had participated, you stated you had not. Both HR and I have reviewed the IM history supplied to us from IT for the past ninety days. I'll ask you again, did you in any way participate and respond to Ted in any type of provocative way during work hours when the subject matter of the interaction was not work related?

Sue (squirming in her chair, wringing her hands, and eyes downcast): I'm not sure what you are asking me.

Sue's manager: If I were to show you or read you an exchange, would that refresh your memory?

Sue: Look, I just wanted Ted to stop. I came in here to get help. I don't know why you just didn't talk with him and ask him to stop sending me messages! Why did you have to dig around? My husband was getting suspicious and asking me a lot of questions because Ted started calling me on my cell after hours. I got scared and he wouldn't listen. At first, I really loved the attention. It was flattering, but after awhile, I didn't know what to do!

Sue's manager: Sue, thank you for finally telling the truth. Unfortunately, your participation over the past three months during work hours, and your failure to be open and honest with HR when you first came in, goes against our policy of integrity and against our systems policy. These violations are serious, and for these reasons, I have no alternative but to immediately terminate your employment. I hope that you learn from these mistakes and that you will not repeat them in your next opportunity. HR will handle your exit from the business. I wish you well in your next role.

Sue: NO! What will I tell my husband? Are you paying me severance? I need to be able to tell him something!

HR specialist: Sue, this is a performance termination and there is no severance offer for lack of performance.

With that, the manager left the office and the HR specialist completed the exit process with Sue. This was a very challenging day for the HR specialist.

The morals of this story:

1. When you are being paid to do a job, do the job.

2. Know your employer's policies and stay within them.

3. Integrity is non-negotiable in the workplace.

4. Nothing is ever "deleted," especially on commercial systems.

5. Workplace behavior counts: sexual conversations and overtures, whether explicit or implied, are always a no-no in a mainstream business environment.

ELEVATOR ANTICS

It was just another annual conference, but a lot seemed to have happened at this particular event. For a start, it was the first one that was not held in the United States, so there were a lot of challenges just in getting people there. The events company, however, had said it was ready for anything—or so they thought!

On the second morning of the event, the head of HR was minding her own business and enjoying breakfast when one of the senior sales leaders approached. He wanted her to know what had happened the night before; he wanted to be the one to tell her, he said. *I can only imagine,* she thought. This guy always had something going on. It seemed that trouble followed him everywhere.

The story went that he got up in the middle of the night to use the restroom. Being in an unfamiliar hotel room and being mostly asleep, it appears that he went to the wrong door and ended up in the hotel hallway, locked out. At this point, he had to admit he sleeps in the buff—of course!

Stark naked with no phone and no key, he started walking towards the elevator to find a house phone. Unfortunately, none was to be found. His next idea was to take the elevator, covering himself as best he could, and go to the front desk for help. Thankfully, the hotel had security cameras in the elevator and lucky (for any unsuspecting guests) hotel security saw him in the buff in the elevator and met him on the ground floor as the doors opened. He explained his plight and was admitted back into his room. No harm, no foul.

However, that wasn't the only misadventure in the elevator that night, and the elevator security camera also caught another inebriated guest urinating in it. *Really?!* thought the head of HR, *he couldn't go to the lobby restroom or wait until he got to his room?* But that wasn't to be the most serious incident that was to happen on that trip; you can read about that in the "Coco Bongo" story.

A HARSH MARKET

The incident described in this story made it all the way to the courthouse. Where should I begin?

Well, once upon a time, there was an opening for a marketing leader at a company. There were three strong candidates and three people on the interview team. The field was narrowed to two candidates, so the interview team met to discuss their final choice. Two of the three were very strongly in agreement to hire one of the candidates, but the third member of the interview team—the HR leader—felt strongly about the other candidate. Against her better judgment, the HR leader acquiesced and ultimately agreed to go with her peers' recommendation. The one quality that had stuck out for them was the candidate's toughness (she had disclosed to them that she was a former high school basketball referee), and this made her especially attractive, given that the marketing team she would be leading was a pretty tough team and fraught with drama.

The woman was appointed and all appeared well. However, toward the end of her first year at the company, there were rumblings of discontent. Inappropriate comments and behaviors by the new leader started to surface. The allegations were numerous, HR investigated just before the year end holiday shutdown. Right after the holidays, several complaints came through to the anonymous hotline about her conduct.

The following allegations were made:

During a company celebration to thank the marketing team, one team member shared with colleagues that she was nervous about her daughter going out on her first date. Allegedly, the marketing leader suggested that the woman advise her daughter to perform a blowjob on her date in order to avoid a full sexual experience. The team member was devastated and felt helpless to respond to her boss in that environment.

At another company event, an employee alleged that, in front of over 300 people, the marketing leader (an openly gay woman), kissed her on the cheek, remarking "I don't know why I just did that" before proceeding to kiss her on the opposite cheek, quite close to her mouth. Once again, this employee was mortified and felt helpless. She was afraid to report it as she felt she would place her job in jeopardy and she needed her job.

The company was involved in an annual bike charity event. The marketing leader allegedly shared with her team that she and her partner had to keep adjusting their bike seats because they were giving them repeated orgasms.

Another incident involved the marketing leader encouraging one of her female employees to pursue a young male coworker because he "was hot." She then retracted her statement, advising the employee to avoid him, as she was concerned he may be "a player" who could have a "sexual disease." She continued to make disparaging comments about the male employee, such as "He's good looking and he knows it," and she said she knew that he "slept around."

Several times the marketing leader also allegedly made her female employees feel uncomfortable by the way she looked at their chests and legs, and by making comments, such as "You look hot today." She would occasionally invite individuals into her office for a meeting, but they never talked about business. Rather, they had to endure uncomfortable stares and inappropriate subjects and comments.

In a meeting about preparing for a large social event, the marketing leader, having never attended this annual event, asked on a conference call if ladies were to "dress hot" for the event. She was quickly admonished by the head of HR who stated that "We don't use the words 'dress hot' for a business function."

During another planning meeting, it was alleged that the marketing leader asked one of her employees if she was sleeping with the CEO's son, also an employee. This was done in front of others and the female employee was visibly shaken. She went on to ask if those two would be sharing a room and if she needed to be aware of anyone else who was sleeping around.

It is alleged that there was preferential treatment of some team members. She had a tendency to "stomp" around the office and to ask, in a very loud voice, where certain employees were. In a cube environment, this was embarrassing and disruptive. It was reported that she violated the personal space of her favorite staff and would reduce the least favored team members to tears. In addition, it was stated that she reveled in publicly berating the non-favored employees on the team. The environment gradually deteriorated, prompting one team member to circulate an article on bullying in the workplace.

A news article in the local paper regarding the Boy Scouts of America's refusal to admit homosexuals became the subject of many conversations in the office. One of the team members was an Eagle Scout, which was known by everyone in the office, and yet the leader would continuously bring up the topics of "gays, girls, and the Godless." These topics are generally taboo for a leader to openly discuss in front of their team members as it could create a hostile work environment given the volatility that are inherent in many of these conversations. There are very strong feelings on both sides of the aisle on these topics, so they are not appropriate conversations to have in the workplace, especially when brought up by a leader.

The difficulty for HR was that the marketing team was divided about the leader (as the interviewers had been): those who supported the leader and those who were intimidated by her. Numerous meetings were held with the marketing leader's manager, the COO, and the head of HR. There are always two sides to every story, and the marketing leader vehemently denied the myriad of allegations. She stated that the individuals making the complaints were poor performers and she just wanted them to do their jobs! She denied the comments and the actions she was being accused of.

When an anonymous complaint was made on two separate occasions, forty-five days apart, two full investigations were carried out. The complaints were exactly the same. Nothing new was reported but a second investigation was completed nevertheless. During the follow-up investigation, the marketing leader once again reiterated that she just needed her people to do their jobs, but she was constantly having to ask them to complete their tasks, even though they were managers or directors on the team. She did not want to lose anyone on the team, just have them be productive.

One of the team members resigned and filed a lawsuit for constructive discharge, claiming he was forced to leave due to a hostile work environment and retaliation by the marketing leader. The case went on for nearly eighteen months before it finally made its way to trial. You might be thinking, based on the allegations, that this would be an open-and-shut case, but the law agrees that there are always two sides to every story!

The jury heard it all from the employee, his wife, other team members, the COO and the head of HR, and others his attorney called upon to testify. At the end of the day, the jury found in favor of the defendant, which was the company. It is believed that they relied on two things: first, the jury believed that the marketing leader did not want to lose the employee but simply wanted him to do his job; and secondly, the jury felt that he had voluntarily given up a six-figure salary before having another job lined up, and that he had only brought the case because he was now in a very significant financial bind. One piece of evidence that seemed to be critical was the fact that the HR leader advised the manager to terminate the employee; but the manager did not want to do that, she simply wanted him to do his job without the "drama" he brought to the team. The jury then saw this as not being constructive discharge or retaliation as he chose to depart.

These are very tough cases, and you just never know what a jury will decide. It took one afternoon and one morning for the jury to reach a decision. It is said that when the verdict came out, the marketing leader went running and yelling down the halls of the office declaring that she had been vindicated! Not a professional response for sure.

Within four months of the jury verdict, it appeared she

was back to her old tricks. She had a new team, and she just couldn't help herself. The complaints started coming in again, and they could not be ignored. The bullying was back and she had to go. The CEO struggled with the decision, because the marketing leader was a really likable person outside of the work arena, she was a very knowledgeable marketing person; but the company had to protect the business and live its stated values. While it felt harsh, it was the right thing to do to make a change in leadership for the good of the marketing team and to protect the organization from further legal exposure.

HIDDEN CAMERA

This story involves a male employee who was having some marital troubles. Somehow, his wife had learned that he visited a strip club while on a company trip with some of his teammates. As it turned out, this guy liked strip clubs and this was not his first visit; he was visiting these clubs while his wife was home with the children. Needless to say, that did not sit well with his wife, and she decided to leave him.

Weeks later, the employee asked a colleague to pick up a client at the airport. The colleague declined. This did not bode well for this colleague, who did not get on well with the guy.

Shortly after this rebuffed airport-run request, there was a dinner attended by this disgruntled employee, some other coworkers, and vendor partners. From information received, the strip-club visiting employee made some disparaging remarks about his colleague in front of the vendor. Other employees heard the remarks and, of course, word got back to the colleague who then filed a complaint with the HR team. After each person present was questioned, it was determined that the incident had violated the company value of respect for the individual.

The manager of the offending employee wanted to have a serious conversation with him and the colleague he had offended to let them know they needed to find a way to get along, be professional, and abide by the company values. He told the pair that that type of behavior was totally unacceptable and would not be tolerated. After the conversation, the manager felt like he had gotten through to them.

Well, not so fast! About two weeks later, the offended colleague got a frantic call from his wife asking him to get home immediately. She refused to tell him what the problem was, but she was clearly terrified and highly emotional. He left the office in a panic. When he arrived home, his wife met him with a letter that had been left on the garage door. The letter told her that she might want to know her husband had visited a strip club at the last sales meeting.

The employee was livid and immediately denied the allegation. He consoled his wife as best he could. Then he quickly realized he had video surveillance on the house. Well, you've guessed it, the video showed pretty clearly that the truck outside of the house and the man walking up his driveway was the strip-club visiting employee! The man was angry, incredulous, and he spilled the beans to his wife about all that had transpired in the last month with this person. He adamantly denied going with this guy to the strip club, alleging this was simple retaliation as he would not be this guy's puppet at work. He sent text messages to his colleagues letting them know what was going on because they were quite worried when he departed for home that day.

Of course, a call was made to HR. The video was shared with the HR leader who had no doubt that it was the employee in question. A phone call was made to the employee, and he was told to watch the surveillance video. He denied it was him in the footage. But he also stated that his windshield had just been broken—he said he wasn't accusing anyone but thought it was an interesting coincidence. He was asked to share a photo of the windshield, but the nick in the windshield was barely visible. He was put on administrative leave with pay while the entire situation was investigated.

HR made calls to each of the employees in that small office. The video was shared with each of them, and they were asked their opinion on who was on that tape. It was unanimous. They all identified the truck and the person walking up the driveway. Interestingly, one of the employees stated that others were afraid of this guy because he had been seen at a bar where he "beat the shit out of guy and walked away as if nothing happened." This guy shares his entire life with the office, and he had shared that he was caught cheating on his wife with a stripper. Since his wife packed up and left with the two children, this guy had been a hostile, angry person.

After speaking with each employee, it was quite clear that this man had driven to his colleague's house, left a threatening note on the garage door, and walked away. It was simply stupid. He had no idea that the employee had a video system on his house! Needless to say he was separated from the company quite quickly, never to be heard from again.

NOT A GOOD DRUNK

Sales events are notorious for celebrating and drinking to excess, and they have been described as college fraternity/sorority parties. This is true no matter the industry. Numerous folks interviewed from a variety of companies have related similar events. Spouses beware!

This story is one of many told to me. A relatively new sales leader was attending his first sales conference. HR received a call during the conference from an individual who had wanted that role, and he reported that the new guy was "drunk, loud, and obnoxious" and had to be carried back to his room by two of his subordinates. The caller went on to state that he had not actually witnessed this but had gotten it third-hand.

HR started making inquiries, and it quickly became clear that there were two camps. Yes, he had a little too much to drink, but no one had to carry him back to his room. He was tipsy, spilled some wine on his shirt … no big deal. He was not loud or obnoxious, and there was no yelling or screaming at the bar.

When they got out into the street, he did yell something in the parking lot as they were headed to the hotel. That was it, they confirmed he got to his room on his own. Was this a case of sour grapes from a man who didn't get the job? The HR person was not sure, so she asked the most senior sales leader to have a chat with this guy to close it out.

The discussion with the new sales leader and the senior sales leader was direct and cordial. The senior guy expressed his dissatisfaction and disappointment about the reported "loud, drunk, obnoxious behavior" at a company event in front of his direct reports. The new guy denied being carried back to his room and stated this has never happened before. He reassured HR that he did not have an alcohol problem and didn't need the employee assistance program. The senior leader let him know that he had the opportunity to prove himself trustworthy to his team and advised him that he should address his behavior directly with them. The new guy thanked his senior leader and committed to never letting this situation happen again.

Fast forward one year …

At the next sales event, the same "reporter" from the year before called HR again. At the sales event, the now not-so-new guy had too much to drink both nights, and he "put the moves on" a colleague's wife at the bar and other women there. It was quite inappropriate and disrespectful. On the second night, the most senior leader of sales pulled the complainant aside and advised him that he had taken care of the prior night's situation.

Later that same night, the same behavior was witnessed. The sales leader was too drunk and asked for assistance to the elevator, as he thought he was going to vomit. The reporter stated his concern was two-fold: (1) Did the guy have a serious drinking problem? and (2) What might the impact be, internally and externally, on the brand, especially with employees who believe this overindulgence is tolerated without repercussions? How is this sales leader expected to gain respect from the staff?

HR talked to other members of staff about the issue. One of the comments received from an employee was that "this guy goes from sober to drunk pretty quickly." The employee also stated that, in his opinion, the sales leader is "not a good drunk" and that whenever the sales leader drank, he got that look in his eyes indicating that he'd had too much, adding: "He becomes quite unprofessional when he drinks, and he probably should not consume alcohol in a business setting as it is reflective and damaging to the company."

It seems that the sales leader was a topic of discussion on mornings after these incidents. People were losing respect for this guy, and he needed help. The "reporter" appears to have been making his own rounds with the staff to investigate whether the guy brought any value to the team, but it seemed that the staff believed him to be a busy body who just wanted the guy out so he could finally get the job he believed should have been his to start with. They all believed the problem was blown out of proportion and was a case of one guy wanting his boss out of the way.

In the middle of all this, it appears that when the team returned from the sales event, they had gotten together to watch the World Series. The sales leader was there but did not touch a drop. When someone commented on this, the sales leader replied, "I have to be on my best behavior."

So was this a case of misconduct or a case of sour grapes? You decide!

RUB AND TUG

A leader's employment was terminated for a variety of infractions. Word was that things were "his way or no way," and he also used profanity on a regular basis to intimidate his employees. A classic bully. He thought he was untouchable; however, at-will employment practices remove a lot of protections, especially for boorish behavior that puts the company at potential risk of harassment and discrimination allegations. Given his arrogance, he filed a wrongful-termination action.

As the case progressed, it became time for depositions. I am not an attorney, but for those not familiar with the legal process, here's a quick explanation: In a civil suit suing for damages, once the actual lawsuit has been filed with the courts and the defendants have been served, there is a process known as "discovery." The first thing that usually happens is the defendant files a response to the "complaint" and both parties then send each other "interrogatories," a series of questions to learn as much as they can about what the other is going to present in court testimony. After that, further discovery includes a "request for a production of documents" (in an employment case these include things like the employment history, performance reviews, a copy of the employee file, etc.). The next item would be the "depositions" of each witness who would be called to testify at trial. This can best be described as a courtroom simulation, in that the witness is testifying under oath in front of a court reporter. Depending on who requested the deposition, that attorney goes first, and then the witness is subject to cross-examination by opposing counsel. The depositions are then transcribed and sent to both parties to certify the accuracy; at that point the documents become a permanent part of the case record and can be referred to at trial.

One of the witnesses in this case was a direct report of the plaintiff (the employee who filed the lawsuit). In most employee relations lawsuits, the head of HR sits in as the company representative. In this case, that is exactly what happened. During the deposition, the questioning turned to an *allegedly* acceptable practice of taking clients to massage parlors for "entertainment." This particular witness, under oath, stated that the plaintiff instructed him to participate and to take a visiting client executive to the "normal location" for this activity. He looked at the HR leader and stated, for the record, that his wife was well aware of this, and while she disapproved, she knew that he did not actively participate with the "massages" and was just the host.

The attorney pressed on and asked him exactly what he meant by not "actively participating in the massage activity." The witness responded that these were not really massages; they were "rub and tugs." The attorney for the plaintiff was really trying his best to embarrass this guy and get him to back down from his willingness to testify. He then asked what a rub and tug was. The poor guy was so embarrassed; he looked at the HR leader and apologized that she would have to hear what he was about to say. He proceeded to describe that a "rub and tug" is a female massaging a certain part of a male's anatomy in order to create a sexual arousal without full intercourse. "You get the picture," said the

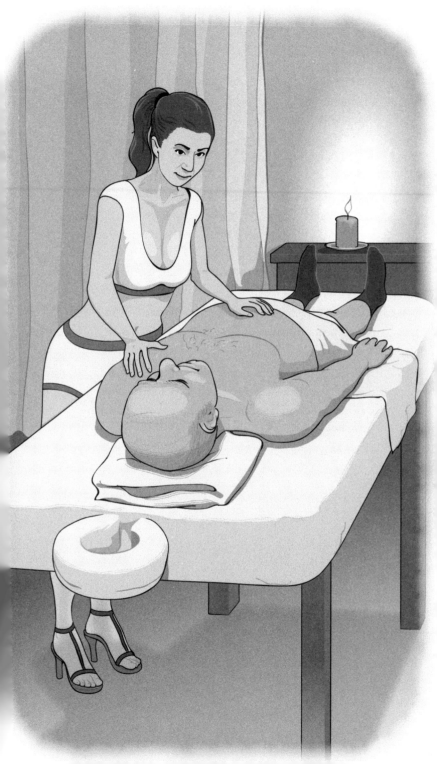

red-faced man, "and that's all I'm going to say about it, except to reiterate that I did not participate in this activity; I was a driver for the client."

As the story goes, immediately after that testimony, the witness asked for a restroom break, which the attorney is required to grant. While on break, the witness approached the HR leader and continued to apologize profusely that she had to hear the testimony, and he hoped that she did not think less of him. He felt trapped because he needed his job, and the plaintiff had been quite threatening, giving him no real choice but to carry out the plan for client entertainment. He further stated that this was a regular course of business.

The HR leader said that this was the first she had ever heard the term "rub and tug," and that every day she learned something knew about human behavior. Ain't that the truth.

It is important to note that after this was all disclosed, the company made it very clear that this behavior and activity was not to be condoned or be a part of client entertainment ever again.

VOMIT COMET

The head of HR and the general counsel did not attend
the annual sales conference that year. They were actually
in another city attending proceedings at a wrongful termination case that was going to trial. The HR leader was the
company representative and the general counsel was there
as a consultant to ensure the outside counsel hired to defend
the company did his job.

One morning, the HR leader received a phone call from
the marketing leader who was managing the sales conference. The marketing leader was quite upset and needed help.
It seems that the company had leased several buses and took
the sales conference attendees to watch the World Series
downtown, away from the hotel, and for dinner and drinks at
various venues around this sports-mad town.

As was to be expected during a major sporting event
in a sports bar, some folks had more than a little too much
alcohol that evening. On one of the bus journeys back to the
hotel (about a forty-minute ride), some were still drinking,
some were singing, and there was plenty of trash talk
to go around!

Well, it wasn't long before someone who'd had too much
to drink, while being jostled around in the back of the bus,
became violently ill. Yes, all over his colleagues! That first
incident started somewhat of a chain reaction, and pretty
soon several people were in on the action. There was vomit

everywhere! One man got "hit" so hard with vomit that he had to take his pants and shoes off and discard them.

The bus driver was angry. Can you just imagine the stench and screaming going on in that bus? He pulled over into a gas station to assess what was going on. When he did, one person started getting loud and obnoxious and making insulting statements about the bus driver, referring to him as one of "those people." The bus driver was the only non-white guy on the bus. The drunk guy then threw up on the exit steps of the bus. Now the bus driver was livid! He demanded to know who was going to clean it up. Of course, people wanted off the bus due to the stench. And then, there were the die-hards who wanted to know if the gas station sold booze.

The obnoxious guy in the front of the bus was on a work visa as a "convenience/accommodation" because his fiancé was transferred to the US on the company L1 visa. He was given a very stern warning that any other infraction would see him heading back to his home country, fiancé or not.

The marketing leader called the head of HR who gave him some guidance. After speaking with nearly everyone on the bus, it was obvious that there was a pact of silence, so the company had to pay the bus company an additional $1500 to clean the bus. Talk about brand recognition: I'm pretty sure that bus company still knows the name of that firm! As for the company, this story has become a legend and is still talked about today! I have been asked numerous times if this story will be in the book!

BAR BILL

It was time to plan the annual sales event. The company used a professional events company that worked with the marketing team to put on this event for 800–1000 employees in sales and sales support. At the time, the company was searching for a new marketing leader and they assigned the communications director to the task of doing site visits with the event planner. The communications director brought along a temporary contractor to assist.

Upon arriving at the site, the host sales director invited the two to have a drink on her at the bar since they had arrived early for the scheduled 5:30 p.m. meeting. Later that afternoon, the event planner arrived on site and met up with them at the bar. She was a little surprised that alcohol was being consumed so early in the day and prior to the important planning meeting, which would entail a lot of attention to detail and require everyone to be on their game. The event planner told them she was going to her room and would see them at the meeting when they should be ready for a solid planning discussion.

The meeting went along without a hitch. They got a lot done and went their separate ways after a quick dinner.

However, that night, when the bill arrived, the company event planner received a call from the host sales director. "I need your help," she said. The planner replied, "Sure, what can I help you with?" The sales director let her know that the communications director and the contractor had run up a $500 bar bill! She further stated that she invited them to have a drink on her, not to consume the entire bar. There wasn't even any food on the bill; it was all booze! The event planner advised the sales director to put the bill on her room and not to worry. The event planner ended up footing the bill because she did not know what else to do; she did not want to throw her client's employee under the bus and she did not want to lose the event.

This particular communications director cooked her own goose in the end because her drinking and expense reports came back to haunt her and she had no one to cover for her like the event planner! She was quickly let go from the business.

IT'S TIME TO MAKE A BABY

The CEO and the COO invited a few senior leaders to a major sporting event. Clients were included and asked into the hospitality tent as well; this was a relatively expensive event, and they were on day two.

One of the senior leaders went to the COO and told him he needed to go home.

"Is everything okay?" the COO asked.

"Yes, but my wife needs me to come home now," the leader replied.

"What's the emergency?"

"Well, if you must know, we've been trying to get pregnant and we are in the ovulation window, so I need to get on a plane."

To the COO's credit, he kept a straight face and wished him luck! So off he went to potentially make a baby and left the client and others standing there.

Who tells their boss these things? The CEO and COO that remained at the event had a good chuckle over that.

FACEBOOK STING

A female employee needed some time off to get her personal life in order. She reported to her manager that her husband had pulled a fast one on her and she got caught.

Her husband learned that she had been having affairs with different men during the recent past. He and his buddy created a fake Facebook page with a profile of one of the men that the husband thought she was pursuing. The page featured the paramour's photo and details, but it was linked to the wronged husband somehow.

Evidently, she took the bait hook, line, and sinker. Unbeknownst to her, she was sending nude photos of herself to her husband, not the man she was pursuing. Her husband had clearly missed his calling as a private eye! Now she was faced with trying to salvage a broken marriage or plan for the divorce. The story goes that she never returned to that company.

People who work in HR wear a variety of hats in support of the staff and the business. Besides handling core HR functions like benefits, compensation, and sometimes payroll, HR also is accountable for attracting, engaging, rewarding, and developing the staff so that the business can thrive and grow. Unfortunately, employees can take up a significant amount of time in HR's day. Don't be the one bringing those non-business challenges into the workplace. Simply agree to do what is expected in the role and do it quite well—if you do so, your career will soar and, in exchange, the company will pay you on time with benefits. It's a win-win proposition and does not include drama! Drama is for TV and the movies; there is no place for it in your work life.

DAMSEL IN DISTRESS

There was once a marketing leader who popped up everywhere a certain sales person seemed to be. They worked in different cities and states. Was it just a coincidence?

The learning and development director was rolling out a new sales leadership training, and the first evening was being combined with a new-hire orientation group to allow for some networking and socializing between colleagues. It made it easier for the executives to be in one place, and it was nice for the newbies to feel very welcomed in their new company.

The HR leader noticed that the marketing director was in attendance at the dinner and inquired why. No one could answer the question. Always concerned about costs and ensuring that the training budget was not abused, the HR leader was confused but let it go so as not to put a damper on the evening.

Later on, the hotel provided the learning and development leader the roster of people who had checked in (the rooming list determined how many rooms the company would be paying for) and any no shows who did not call by 6:00 p.m. to cancel. The marketing leader did not appear on the rooming list. The learning and development leader went to the HR leader and shared this information with her. What should she do? The answer was simple: ask her where she is staying!

When the inquiry was made, it was learned that she was rooming with a friend. "What friend?" the leader wanted to know. She preferred not to say. *Really?* thought the leader. *Well, you know how these things go; the truth always comes out. Let it go for now.*

As the night wore on and the adult beverages flowed, it became quite apparent with whom she was rooming, and she later disappeared with a married sales leader. The learning and development leader once again went to the HR leader. The HR leader said she would handle it.

The next morning, the marketing person did not show up for either the new-hire orientation or the sales leaders sessions. At the break, the HR leader asked to speak to the married sales leader in private. The story he gave was quite tall! He claimed that the marketing leader had maxed out her credit cards and could not attend the training because she could not reserve a room. She was quite embarrassed by that. He told the HR leader that he felt bad for her. Because he really liked her, he had offered to let her share his room!

"Wouldn't it have been better to just offer to pay for her separate room on your credit card?" asked the HR leader, who also wanted to know why she was even in attendance and whether he knew where she was that morning. His story was that she was still in the room because she had had a rough night and was not feeling well.

The HR leader pressed on with questions. Are you involved romantically with her? Are you using company funds for an affair? It seemed that she had made numerous visits to his city and showed up wherever he was. He then said, "I'm going to give it to you straight. She is pursuing me, but we have become just good friends. She is in a tough financial spot because her divorce is tough, and I just wanted to help her out. Nothing more. We are not having an affair. I'm just being a nice guy. I'm married!" The HR leader thanked him for his "honesty" (she used that word loosely) and told him to go back to his session. She further advised that the marketing leader would be sent back to her office and would be gone from his room.

The HR leader then called the room and spoke with her. She was requested to pack her bag and come to the lobby to meet the HR leader for coffee. She was downstairs in fifteen minutes looking quite disheveled. The HR leader inquired why she had chosen to come to a meeting that she had not been invited to. The response was that she thought it would be good to spend time with the new hires and to learn some things about sales in the sales leader sessions. Her boss had approved her attendance.

The HR leader then advised her that sharing a room with a male leader who was married was totally unprofessional and unacceptable in the company culture. There were other options available to her. She stated she didn't want the entire company to know of her financial situation. Not an acceptable excuse! The HR leader then advised that her attendance for the remaining two days was not needed and she could get in her car and drive the four hours back to her office. Furthermore, she needed to have a conversation with her manager about future travel and how she would get it covered, given her financial situation, but rooming with the opposite sex was not an option.

The sales leader was quite concerned about his reputation with the HR leader and asked to speak with her again at lunch. He didn't want his career hurt because he had made a poor decision. He also was concerned about who else would "find out" about this. She responded, "You needed to be concerned about that long before this conversation!"

It is believed that it was a short affair because he was definitely more concerned about himself than really helping a damsel in distress! Human behavior is just so fascinating, and people really believe they can get one over on others, but deceit always loses in the end. There are always people watching what's going on, especially when someone is talking to the HR leader. They make up stories in their minds and then tongues start wagging.

Both parties eventually left the company. A loss all around.

BASIC INSTINCT

These stories are all related to one employee, nicknamed Blondie, who created bedlam wherever she went. She traveled a lot in her job, so she left chaos in her wake all over the country. It has become fodder for many storytelling nights at this company, or so I'm told.

There was a major company event at a very nice hotel in a large, popular city during the height of the bed-bug epidemic. Blondie decided to have some fun and started a bed-bug rumor, creating a lot of havoc within an already stressed hotel and hassle for the event planner. No bed bugs were found in the search anywhere in the hotel. Much ado about nothing.

Blondie showed up at another event with no suitcase. She only had the clothes she was wearing. Unfortunately, she was wearing a very short denim skirt without underwear! Think of the Sharon Stone scene in *Basic Instinct*. Well, if that wasn't bad enough, the next day her skirt was found in the event planning "war room." A call was made by her to the event planning company to please send someone to buy her some clothes. And as all good partners would do, they took care of the client's needs.

At that same event, she had a case of beer delivered to her room and was not seen for two days. She was on the corporate team that was hosting the event! Do you know the best way to cover up how much alcohol you have ordered?

Apparently, the scheme is to get to the bar early, drink to your liver's capacity, and when people show up, you start ordering a bunch of food whether they want it or not. It makes it appear that there was a large crowd there and the amount of alcohol on the bill is not questioned. Yep, that was one of this individual's games she liked to play when traveling with others.

INEBRIATED COVER-UP

Somehow, a known alcoholic had the opportunity to pitch a sale to a very important client. The source of this particular story had known this salesperson for over ten years; he was actually his former brother-in-law (both had been married to sisters). The two were tasked to pitch a solution to a client together, and at that point, the known alcoholic had been dry for nearly two years.

A marketing event was planned. About fifteen people were to attend, and it was set up and pre-paid to about the tune of $3000. The day before the event, a call was placed to the "recovering alcoholic" to make sure all was in order for the event the following day. It was three o'clock in the afternoon and he was at the bar, inebriated. Evidently, he didn't go home the night before and his wife tossed him out! He was to be the only presenter at the event. The brother-in-law went to get him at the bar and reported, "Yep, he's as drunk as a puddle."

"Are you going to be okay for tomorrow?" he asked.

"Fuck, yeah! I'll be fine. The boss is fine, everyone's fine!" came the slurred reply.

Well, brother-in-law did not agree and started to plan. He finally got the drunkard into the car and back to the hotel to try to dry him out so that they could go over the presentation together. All the while, he was sending out mayday calls for help! When he got him to the hotel, the brother-in-law's phone rang and he learned that the guy's wife had arrived at the bar and was demanding to know where he had gone.

"His car is here!" she screamed. "If he shows up, tell him he's going to be arrested!"

Someone got his car moved to the hotel and kept the keys. His bag was taken to the reception and given to staff at the front desk. The receptionist started to dial his room, but the brother-in-law stopped her and asked her to wait until he had departed, as he did not want to get tangled up with him. He told her to tell the guy that he would be back to get him at 7:00 a.m. "Please deliver the bag to his room so he doesn't see the bar again!" he said.

The next day, someone else drove three hours to make the presentation. He was not told why he had to do it last minute, just that he had to be there to impress a "most valued client."

The brother-in-law was still worried that the guy was going to start drinking again. He went to the hotel to give him the keys to his car. Shortly thereafter, the guy called his brother-in-law: "This is the worst day of my life. I'm getting separation papers." The brother-in-law thought he was getting separated from the company and replied, "Don't worry, I'll help you make the best of it. You can build your network for your next job. Between the two of us, we have plenty of contacts."

"What are you talking about?" said the guy. "I'm still employed! It's my wife that is serving me separation papers!"

He had no money to even pay for the hotel, so the soon-to-be ex-brother-in-law took care of the hotel. "Please just hold it together until we get done with this client!" he pleaded. It was explained to the client that the employee had taken ill, so another colleague would be making the presentation, and the account was saved ... not without a lot of stress and craziness in the process.

COCO BONGO

Full disclosure on this one: I was steered away from going to Coco Bongo on this trip! This is a true story, although the names are definitely omitted to protect the guilty.

After the awards night, there was always an after party with alcohol and dancing. Everyone knows what happens when celebrating and partying are put together when you are away from home. The after party really was a lot of fun; people were happy, letting their hair down and having a laugh, usually after a really tough year in sales. I was no exception, and I had probably consumed at least one glass of wine too many. The party ended and people were either headed back to their rooms or getting on a bus to the after-after party at a night spot called Coco Bongo.

One of the leaders came up to me and said: "Come with us, we are going downtown!" Another wise leader heard this and said to me: "I don't think that's a good idea. I'm happy to walk you to your room." He walked me back to my room and that was it: goodnight!

The next morning, the crowd that went to the Coco Bongo looked pretty rough, but most of them did show up for the morning session. One of the stories that leaked out was about a very attractive female employee who was evidently quite good at pole dancing, who performed for her fellow colleagues. The guys were quite happy to have witnessed that.

It took quite a few more years—yes, years—for the story

of an arrest to come out. It seems that one of the employees found himself in a jail cell (in a foreign country) and needed bail money to get out! Of course, a call went out to the event planner for help. Evidently, a collection was taken up to get him out, and he found his way back to the conference.

I nearly died laughing when the story finally made it back to me. The folks went to great lengths to keep this story away from the HR leader! It really was a good thing I did not get on that bus...

I'm quite confident that there are many other stories that were kept from me over the years. I'll never really know for sure!

IT'S NOT ALWAYS BLACK AND WHITE

There was a conference that several staff members were to attend so that they could work the company's display booth. At some point, the team ended up at the bar, and one of the young women had too much to drink. She asked her colleague, a young man who had been with the firm for several years, to walk her back to her room. He agreed, and when they arrived at her room, she realized she did not have her key. He took her to his room and left her there while he went to the front desk to get a replacement key. Of course, they would not just give him a key, so he asked if they would accompany him to get her from his room to her room and give her the key.

When they arrived back at the room, she was sleeping on one of the queen beds. The hotel employee and the coworker woke her and escorted her to her room. All was good, and he went back to the conference.

The next day, she accused her coworker of assaulting her in his room. She stated that she woke up on his bed and felt something hard against her. She said she pretended to be asleep and he left. The next thing she remembered was waking up in her own hotel room.

This was brought to the head of the firm. The head of the firm wanted no part of a sexual assault allegation in the firm, and this young man was seemingly being marked guilty without an investigation. The office manager told her boss she would get to the bottom of this. "He's been a great employee for over five years," she said. "He's engaged to be married, he's a true gentleman in every way, and he is well-respected in the firm." She was given the green light to sort it out. Technically, this should have gone to HR to sort out, not the office manager who was not trained in workplace investigations.

The office manager first spoke with the accused, and he relayed his side of the story. He didn't know what the woman meant by "something hard," but he said he always put his suitcase on the extra bed in a hotel room. Perhaps, he surmised, she passed out while he was gone and simply felt the suitcase on her back. He had no idea what had happened, but he knew he had not assaulted her; he was not interested in her, he had not been drinking, and he was true to his fiancé.

The office manager then called the hotel and spoke with the person who helped him. She also had them pull the hallway videotapes. Upon review of the tapes, it was a matter of seconds from when the two entered his room and he departed to fetch the hotel clerk. When the two men entered the room, only a few seconds passed before they exited the room and took the woman down the hall, depositing her at the door to her room. There was no way in that short time that anything could have happened, she surmised.

The office manager shared all of this with the female employee and asked her what she saw and thought. She was quite embarrassed and apologized for jumping to conclusions. This created a real challenge for the two colleagues to be able to work together again, and she left the firm shortly thereafter. Besides the wrong accusation, what in the world was she doing getting inebriated while she was supposed to be working the booth?

The young man thanked the office manager for believing in him. Just an example of how quickly people jump to conclusions and become the judge and jury without a proper investigation. This happens everywhere in life. Fortunately, this guy was exonerated quickly.

LIQUID LUNCH

This story took a few days to come to the attention of the HR leader, and it is an example of guys who abandon their friends in the workplace, especially when they are also guilty of contributing to the problem.

Three employees went out for lunch in a city where everyone knows everyone and antics are usually witnessed and become the subject of office banter. Apparently, one of the three men had a liquid lunch and made the mistake of coming back to the office. The inebriated buddies picked up their belongings from their desks and headed out, leaving him drunk in the office, unable to even keep his head up. Now that's true friendship for you! Evidently the alcohol had really hit him hard after he returned to the office; he could not walk or get out of the chair. One of his colleagues who sat on the other side of the cubicle wall heard him at his desk. He heard a loud crash, and when he checked it out, he found the guy "flat on the floor on his back with his feet on the desk"!

Well, there was a client in the office and, of course, this behavior had to be hidden from view. The employee helped the drunk guy get up, but he wouldn't leave the office. "It's in your best interest to get out of here!" the helpful employee told him, but the guy just sat there. The employee then sent text messages to the two drinking buddies, asking them to come back and help get him out of the office. No deal.

The front desk person and another colleague further tried to help by offering to get him into a cab. He refused. He headed down the hall, and one of his colleagues noted he did not appear "to have his wits about him." The manager of these three was nowhere to be found (and in fact, could not be reached for a few days!). The colleague and another person in the office tried to get him on a train, and in the end, it took four employees to achieve this feat. He was last seen getting on the train and the train doors closing behind him. Potential office crisis averted!

However, that is not the end of the story. Two individuals from the company's top partner saw him on the train. He got into some kind of incident and was asked to leave the train at the next stop. The partner reported that the employee had gotten "out of control" because he thought he was on the wrong train. The next day, one of the managers in the company received a call from the partner who relayed what he had seen and wanted to ensure that the guy made it home okay.

Of course, readers will know by now who got the next call! The investigation by HR revealed the story that has been retold so far, but the conversation with the employee shed new light.

The employee stated he'd had a rough reporting period and was disappointed with his results. The three guys went to a late lunch, and he incorrectly decided to have a "few" drinks. He probably should not have returned to the office, but he did. He disclosed that the total bill for the three was $370—that was for lunch! He recalls interacting with a few folks while he was in the office and had since apologized to each of them. He stated only one person helped him to the train. He believed he wasn't too drunk and felt he must be entitled to "one strike." Fortunately for this guy, he wasn't fired, but he was given a one-time warning. He ended up leaving the firm soon after. And, oh by the way, he was told he could not expense that lunch!

PARTYGATE

What's a holiday party without drama or regrettable behavior? This particular company thought they were smart to try and limit the alcohol intake of party goers by giving each employee two drink tickets, and the leaders four tickets (the thought being that they could pass out tickets as they moved around the room chatting with folks, sort of a recognition/thank you by the top leaders). What they didn't plan for was non-drinkers giving their tickets to others. You probably can guess where this story is going!

One young lady had been given a number of tickets, and it was said that she was heavily intoxicated. She left the building and someone brought her back in. Later on, the party moved from one bar to another, and no one stopped her or anyone else from driving. At the second bar stop, she (and others) continued drinking. One of the mid-level leaders started buying shots. A licorice flavored shot was handed to one of the top guys who refused it, saying, "I don't like those." He later told the HR leader that he refused as he knows what happens after liquor shots start.

Two of the senior leaders reported (later) that it seemed folks were trying to get the senior team "loaded." One of the senior leaders was seen giving the young lady a hug as she left the first stop, and then later it was reported that he also said something inappropriate to her. The other senior leader stated that he had his own barometer of when it was time to leave events such as this, and he left without saying anything to anyone. When he left, he did not recall anyone being out of control; he just knew it was time for him to go. He did hear some stories the next morning, but he wasn't there and would not be able to substantiate the stories. The only story he could substantiate was that the head of finance got stuck with the bill!

Another leader that HR spoke with said that nothing really happened, although he felt like the employees were hanging around to "take them (the senior leaders) down." He later changed his story slightly. He recalled a young female "buzzing around" the executive team—he didn't know her name, she just seemed to be hanging around them—and he believed that at least one member of the executive team had had too much to drink. This guy took the exec back to the hotel (admitting that he probably shouldn't have been driving either).

The young lady who had been buzzing around had a boyfriend who started texting members of her team at 3:30 a.m. that night wanting to know where she was. They simply responded that they last saw her at the party. As it turns out, she was passed out in the parking lot in her car. He found her there, and her car was unlocked—quite a dangerous position for a young, attractive lady to be in.

When HR chatted with her, she added a new twist to the stories coming out of that night. She stated that one of the executives who'd had quite a bit to drink started coming on to her just after midnight. He told her, "Oh God, you're beautiful" and gave her his room number. She said that she told him no because "you're married" before she walked away and went to another of the executives whom she felt "safe" chatting with. She asked the second exec if he would be able to stop the other guy from coming on to her. In speaking with him later, he, of course, denied that this conversation ever took place.

One of her female colleagues stated something different, however. She said that this young woman was aggressively pursuing the guy she reportedly felt "safe" with, and he was backing away from her. Two of the other male colleagues had to come to his rescue.

You can derive your own conclusions about what happened that night. As it turns outs, no formal complaints were filed and life moved on. It was explained to her that her story could not be corroborated and that, in fact, one of her colleagues disputed her version. She told HR that she just wanted to put this behind her and get back to work. She actually left the firm not long after that and was never heard from again. The HR person said she was glad to have dodged a bullet because this could have kept the HR and legal team busy for a very long time.

CULTURE CLASH

Company acquisitions are generally challenging. You read about them on the news, and it looks so easy: Company X is now owned by company Y, and life appears to go on. But it's not easy if you are on the "inside" of the acquisition! This story is about some added "spice" that was added to one particular acquisition.

There's always what is known as "due diligence" before an acquisition is completed. This is when the acquiring company sends in an undercover team so as not to spook the current staff. On its mission, the team tries to learn all it can about the company they are acquiring. Those involved on both companies' teams sign confidentiality agreements under threat of termination if they leak what they are doing to anyone inside or outside of the organization. Due diligence is much deeper than whether or not they are profitable, have pending litigation against them, whether they are carrying any debt, and so on; there's always a question about whether the companies are a cultural fit with each other.

After this particular acquisition, the culture clash started to appear too late. Once all the documents were signed, the real owners started to disclose what it was really like working at the company they had built. While there were subtle hints during the due diligence period at various dinners, the owners of the company turned out to be quite the party animals, but the depth of the partying was never really detailed. As it turned out, they were quite proud of the drunken events with their employees. In addition, there were quite a few compromising relationships that could have been legally risky. Integration had not really started yet, but the money had exchanged hands and so the deal was done.

At the first event for a regional sales recognition, red flags went up pretty quickly during a pontoon boat ride. There were two HR people on the boat from the acquiring company, and the rest were from the acquired company. A few of the folks got on the boat with a 1.5 liter bottle of wine and a few cups. They had no intention of sharing! They had obviously been imbibing for a while and were quite loud in their storytelling. The gist of the story was about where they lived, who in the office lived near them or in the same complex, and who was "banging" who. Not exactly the type of conversation that one would expect to experience at a company sanctioned function, especially knowing that HR people were on the boat! One of the people involved in the conversation was a supervisor in the acquired team, which put additional risk on the newly merged business because the staff were using such inappropriate language and innuendo.

The following day, one of the HR people spoke with their HR leader and learned that this was normal conversation and "that's how it is in this company: Anything goes!" This was the first real experience of a culture clash within these two entities that were now joined.

Throughout the coming weeks, immediately after the close, more was learned about the culture clash. One significant clash emerged at the "Lone Tree" annual weekend event. The craziness that took place was usually so significant that the acquired company had to put down a $10,000 deposit to cover any potential damages by the attendees! It was said that about 30 percent of the company attended (no spouses or significant others), and they took over this small town for a weekend of alcohol, games, alcohol, golf, alcohol … you get the picture. Most people could not remember what they drank or what they did over the weekend, but the photos that leaked out jogged a few memories. (In another chapter in this book, you read about the coffee mug photo—that was taken on one of these weekends.)

Well, the acquired company wanted to do one more of these "Lone Tree" weekends after the merger. However, it was made blatantly clear that this was not a company sanctioned event. In fact, the prior owners actually paid for the event with their own money, that's how much they wanted to have the final soiree! While there are a few stories from that weekend, most were kept secret because "what happens in Lone Tree stays in Lone Tree." One story that came out was an actual fist-fight between drunken coworkers from the same team. After the weekend fight, the "victim" of the attack wanted HR's help because he did not want to work with this guy anymore and wanted HR to get the aggressor removed from the team! It was explained to him that this occurred off the clock, and while the behavior described is not in keeping with the company values, the company was not going to make personnel changes based on behavior at a non-sanctioned event he voluntarily attended knowing some of the behaviors that were acceptable at Lone Tree but totally against company policy in the work environment.

The aggressor apologized several times and was remorseful, but the "victim" was not interested in his apology. They were told that they didn't have to like each other, but while at work, they had to be respectful of each other. Eventually, they both left the organization.

One interesting comment that came later was that the acquisition had taken all of the fun out of working at the acquired company! They accused the acquiring company of being boring and lacking the ability to really know how to have fun at work and with your colleagues. Really?! You have to get drunk, make a spectacle of yourself, get into fights, and act like the characters in *Animal House* to enjoy your workplace and your colleagues? Good grief!

ALCOHOL POISONING

A member of a hotel's cleaning staff knocked on the door to complete housekeeping duties and got no reply. She entered the room to find a male lying across the bed, fully clothed. He did not appear to be alive. She called for security and they rushed to the room. He was breathing, but he was totally out of it and had vomited and was actually sleeping in his own vomit. They called 911, and he was taken to the hospital.

Meanwhile, his company was looking for him. They knew he was traveling, but he did not show up at the client's site and was not answering his cell phone. They tried one more time, and someone answered the phone who identified himself as a manager at the hotel. That is how the company learned of this guy's whereabouts.

The employee's manager called HR for guidance. The HR person said he would take it from there and called the emergency number contained in the employee's file. He spoke with the employee's spouse and let her know her husband had been taken to the hospital for an unknown reason. The spouse was given the information on the hospital and asked to let HR know what she learned about the employee's condition.

Several hours later, HR was notified that the employee had been released, had returned to the hotel to get his things, and was headed home. The spouse said she would have the employee call HR when they arrived home.

It appeared that the employee had imbibed too much the night before in the hotel bar, and had to be helped to his room, where he simply passed out! Upon getting to the hospital, dehydration had set in and the employee was pumped with fluids and sent on his merry way. Evidently, the employee was so dehydrated that his blood pressure was dangerously low. He didn't even remember the ambulance ride!

That employee escaped a nasty fate and was very lucky that he had not put the "Do Not Disturb" sign on the hotel door. Saved by housekeeping, but not saved from the wrath of his boss and spouse!

JUDAS

For those of you who study the Bible, you know the story of Judas denying three times that he knew Jesus. Well, this VP's responses to questions from his boss were similar to Judas's responses to the High Priest Caiaphas.

It was learned that a VP might be having a relationship with an administrative assistant. His boss called him in to chat about it.

Boss: "Do you know her?"

VP: "Yes, she's a friend. There's no relationship."

Boss: "That's it?"

VP: "Yes, we had dinner."

Boss: "You dined with her when she lives in another state?"

VP: "She came to my city, but lots of people come to my city."

Boss: "Anything you remember about the dinner?"

VP: "Well, I kissed her."

Boss: "Anything else?"

VP: "Okay, we had a relationship. I shouldn't have let it get out of hand."

Boss: "Why didn't you just say that to start with?"

VP: "I knew it was against policy as a senior leader."

Boss: "I have zero tolerance for unprofessional behavior, especially at the senior leadership level. In your role this type of transgression is inexcusable."

The VP was given the opportunity to resign or be terminated. He wanted to chat with an attorney first, but he then changed his mind and resigned on the spot. This was not his first rodeo—rather, it was the straw that broke the proverbial camel's back during his tenure.

DRINKS WITH THE BOSS

An attractive, single female employee got an email from a senior leader inviting her to his room after 10:00 p.m. for a drink. She was so "weirded out," she wanted to throw her computer. This guy was very senior in the company and twenty-five years older. She had been working hard at the conference all day and was tired. She called one of her coworkers and confided in her about the invitation and asked what should she do. Following some advice, she decided to ignore him.

The very next day, this guy was paraded across the stage with the CEO and was showered with accolades about the great work he did for the team and the company. She was creeped out again and became disgusted with all the fuss around this guy. While she listened to the CEO go on and on, she kept thinking, *He's not that kind of guy. You have no idea about him and the email he sent me last night!* This kept burning inside of her. She talked to her two mentors and got it off her chest, and because she was still so upset and it was having an impact on her ability to do her job, they encouraged her to say something to him.

After talking with her mentors, she decided to take action by sending him an email and blind copying one of her mentors. In the email she told him how much he had upset her and about the impact it was having on her, especially considering his role in the company. She went on to ask him how he would have felt if a senior leader had done that to one of his daughters! She kind of let him have it. She just could not let it go.

Several months later, she contacted HR. She was still upset about the incident and really could not let it go, especially because her job required her to have contact with him. She had shared his original email with her mom, who had the same reaction to it, thinking it very creepy, unprofessional, and weird. She told HR she was still embarrassed by this and just wanted it to go away. She didn't like being uncomfortable doing her job and fearing him contacting her for some work that needed to be done. HR reassured her that they would look into it.

HR determined that this manager's boss should be made aware. He said he sensed something was up with her at the conference, but he assumed it was just the pressure of the event. He was quite disappointed in the man and preferred HR to handle it. He only wanted to get involved if needed.

When HR contacted the offender, he said he had meant nothing by the invitation, and he actually got quite angry when he received her email referring to him as a "creepy old man." He said he had thought that sending the invitation to her work email would be an indicator that it was just a drink with a colleague and nothing more! He said that he was floored when he received the email from her chastising him for the invitation.

He offered to apologize again. The HR person thought that would be fine, but to do so verbally and stay off email. The HR person also advised him to think more than twice before sending an email to a junior female inviting them to his room, regardless of his good intentions, because it created a risk to the organization and could create a hostile work environment for the female.

The executive said he would never do it again and felt bad that she was so upset. He knew something was wrong between them the next day, but he never connected the email to her behavior towards him. Was he really that naïve or did he just put on a convincingly innocent defense? Only he knows the answer to that!

The woman involved continued to be frustrated by the whole thing, could not let it go, and chose to leave the company. The company lost a great employee due to a significant executive error in judgment. He should have known better. There had not been a prior allegation, so the decision was made that this was his one error, and he knew he was now on thin ground. He also left the organization a short time later.

FIGHT!

At the annual conference, one of the top guys in engineering was set to receive a CEO Award for his accomplishments during the year. It was a prestigious award. This engineer was a "lead engineer" and a member of the leadership forum group.

The story goes that during the afternoon of the awards night, he had been imbibing. He and one of the top sales guys had both been bending their elbows at the bar and had done a few too many arm exercises that afternoon. One thing led to another and they started arguing—over what it was never made clear!

Pretty soon, they got so heated that the engineer asked the sales guy to "step outside" and he'd settle the dispute once and for all. Other folks saw and heard this and went looking for someone to help cool them down. Well, that did not go over too well and it took more than a little encouragement to get them to stop. Not a great display of professionalism from the engineer! He was not someone the CEO now wanted to bring onto the stage to recognize his leadership and accomplishments.

So, there was a huddle and a decision made that the award would go to the runner-up that year and this guy needed to be taught a lesson on leadership. He was provided the feedback; he was apologetic and also apologized to the sales guy once they both sobered up. They actually apologized to each other and to the executive team for their behaviors. Over-indulging in alcohol really does impact careers.

REVENGE & RETALIATION

CREATIVE ALIMONY

An employee came to his manager asking to be moved from an employee W2 status to a contractor 1099 status. When asked why, he said, "I need to avoid paying alimony. At my salary, having to produce a W2 will kill me."

His manager could not believe it. He explained all of the legal reasons why it couldn't be done while also tiptoeing around the integrity issues. In addition, he tactfully tried to advise the employee not to bring personal challenges into the workplace and suggested that there was perhaps a better way to approach the problem.

The employee became angry and threatened to quit. The manager did some back-pedaling, because losing him would leave the company exposed with the client. Of course, the next call went to the HR team who also had to involve legal. The only way was if he formally resigned and started his own company; then he could be hired back as a contractor.

He was going to have to think about that because it would require getting licensed, insured, and bonded. He thought he may just have to pay the alimony.

Unfortunately, a few weeks later, he resigned because he found another company that would take him on as a contractor without all the legal requirements his current company had put in his path. Not the resolution the manager wanted, but the company was adamant that they were not interested in playing legal games that could expose them to repercussions by the IRS or Federal employment laws in the future.

The lengths people go to in order to avoid meeting their obligations!

REVENGE BEDLAM

One day, an HR leader goes to see the CEO. A large distribution center has a problem, and she doesn't know what to do. It seems that the top sales manager and one of his direct reports were caught having an affair. The CEO was surprised to hear this news. The sales manager's wife is also an employee of the company, so how stupid could this guy be? The CEO wants the opportunity to talk with the sales manager himself.

The CEO calls in the sales manager, tells him what he has heard, and asks for verification. He gives the sales manager the advice to think twice about lying to him. After a few minutes of deep thought, the sales manager comes clean. Yes, it is true. He is not in love with his employee; he was only sleeping with her to get even with someone.

The CEO is incredulous. He put the company at risk to seek revenge? Who might he be seeking revenge against that he needs to risk not only the company but his very own livelihood? The sales manager is hesitant to share that piece of information, but, getting irritated, the CEO informs him he needs to come clean and do so pretty quickly. Can you imagine the CEO's face when he finally learns that the sales manager's wife is also having an affair? It seems the employee had wanted to level the playing field!

Well, you really can't make this shit up, thinks the CEO. But it gets worse.

You might be curious as to who the wife was having an affair with—the CEO certainly was. But he couldn't believe the truth: It was with the decision-maker of the company's top client. Yes, the man who was key to the largest revenue stream in the CEO's geographic territory! What's a CEO to do?

The most interesting part of this story to me is that the CEO got no guidance or legal advice from the HR leader. What she should have told him was that the company was registered in an at-will employment state and that the company had a policy requiring employees to disclose a personal relationship with another employee. Not one but two reasons that could have made this an easy problem to resolve.

After speaking with the woman in the scenario, the CEO learned that she and the client were more than lovers; she was prepared to leave her husband and, if necessary, would leave the business. Both she and the CEO knew that having a personal relationship with a client might lead to assumptions of favoritism and could have legal implications, regardless of whether they truly loved each other.

The CEO really struggled with this one. He lost a lot of sleep. The sales manager was one of his best. There was also the risk that the salesperson with whom the sales manager was having a revenge affair could allege quid pro quo (this for that), putting the company in a legal bind, and it could lose its largest account!

Fortunately for this CEO—and it rarely works out so well— the client liked the company's products and services and he loved the wife! She agreed to leave the business (and her husband), and the CEO re-assigned the account to another sales manager. The vengeful sales manager received a one-time warning and the female salesperson with whom he was having the affair was re-assigned. Of course they broke up after she learned she was being used! But for her, this story has a happy ending because after she was re-assigned, she received one or two lucrative accounts that significantly increased her income (one might conclude that this was a form of "hush" money).

I can tell you, this course of action is not what I would have recommended, but it worked for this CEO. When I interviewed him, he was quite proud that he was able to settle this craziness without it really costing his company any money—he certainly dodged a mighty big bullet!

THREE MUSKETEERS

This matter went on for weeks and consumed a ton of the HR team's time. None of it would have been necessary if people knew how to listen and solve problems together, rather than pointing fingers and creating drama where none should exist.

This situation occurred in a software company and involved an international deployment of a direct customer interface. It had nothing to do with a life-saving software; no lives were at risk with this system. There may be some customer challenges as a result of the rollout, but certainly nothing that could not be handled professionally.

Apparently, there was a bug in the system that kept a confirmation button from popping up and letting the user know that their request had gone through. Normally, it would be a low priority, but this particular customer created such drama that it became a high priority when the situation escalated. The response time and what the responders did were completely documented, but it was not enough for the manager, who was all over the team. He became out of control with concern about how these things were being tracked.

The team leader was called in and raked over the coals by the developer, the developer's boss, and her boss. She felt totally blindsided and bullied by these three guys. HR's one-on-one with her revealed that, in her opinion, the guys were known by the larger team as the Three Musketeers, led by the software developer, even though he was not an actual employee. Everything had to be done his way, and the company leader did not exert any power over the contractor. The broader company saw the full team as "elitist"; the leader of the team was seen as the "figure-head," and the software leader was seen as the "brains."

At one point in the discussion, the situation sounded almost like a doomed Apollo space mission. The team did not want to deploy the software because there were too many risks, but a decision was made to move forward anyway, which resulted in an error that the client saw before it could be fixed.

The team leader said she needed to be able to access information from the Three Musketeers without fear of retaliation. She wanted them to solve the problems she brought to their attention and to stop blaming her for everything that happened. "They spend more time trying to figure out who made an error than they do on diagnosing and fixing the problem!" she said.

In speaking with other team members who interacted with the team, a different picture was painted. The picture became blurred and abstract. Many discussions with her to diagnose and resolve problems became heated discussions because she was considered defensive and territorial. It was noted by many that she did not have the technical expertise to assist in the diagnosis of software bugs, and this made the work even more challenging for those trying to fix problems. The other teams felt that she focused on completing Service Level Agreements in a timely fashion, when what they really needed her to do was help really solve difficult challenges so that the problems didn't occur.

In addition, she seemed to have a real challenge in hiring the right staff, and people believed that was also a direct result of not being tech-savvy. This had a negative impact on the product and the service delivery to customers. She was also described as stubborn and having an inability to accept direction and feedback.

Other workers commented that her team did not listen well and failed to check all the facts before raising the matter to a higher level, matters that could have been handled and closed without the escalation. The workers did not like to bring up issues, as it generally ended in an argument. They became tired of the conflict and wanted to just help the customers. The word was that her team was right and everyone else was wrong.

Evidently, working with her became so difficult that some just gave up. Sometimes they felt like they were in email hell, caught up in endless email arguments. They asked many times to be taken off the email list but to no avail. One particular meeting was described as "unbearable." The beginning of the meeting was productive, but then she took the floor and did not let anyone else talk for forty-five minutes, and nobody stopped her! (I personally find this amazing and intolerable!). The "figure head" said nothing. It was assumed he was letting her hang herself in front of the others so that he could prove his point that she needed to go.

After all of this fact gathering, the HR person had another conversation with her. As the HR person started to provide the feedback, it became quite clear that the employee was not going to take any accountability for the issues that she was hearing. She became argumentative, and the HR person had to stop her and ask her to just listen for a moment, or

they were going to get nowhere. When the HR person was finished with giving her examples of how the broader group was feeling, the employee said "I knew I wasn't going to be treated fairly. This whole thing is retaliation. You are being unfair and you are trying to build a case against me. I came to HR in the first place, and this has all been turned around on me!" The two talked for quite a long time.

She stated that she was tired. She had worked under duress for a long time with this group. It was time to move on because she would not be able to facilitate the change that she believed needed to happen. (This statement alone may explain some of the challenges she has experienced; it sounded like she was trying to force change and was met with resistance!) She told HR that there were a few individual contributor roles opening up and she planned to apply. She felt a new chapter needed to be written. She said she needed to work in an environment that wasn't so hostile. She said to HR that she had no agenda and was not interested in moving a retaliation claim forward (good thing as it sounds like she had a weak case!), and instead she was going to put her energy into securing a new role.

She wanted advice on how to handle the Three Musketeers until she had secured a new role. The HR person recommended that she practice listening without immediately reacting and work on how she responded to issues. It was suggested that she have one-on-ones with each "Musketeer" to clear the air, letting them know she was planning to move on within the company and ask for their help in the process; in exchange she would stop arguing with them.

The author learned that this person did find another job within the company, it lasted about nine months before she finally left to chase her dream. The Three Musketeers celebrated, but no swords were drawn in this story.

OFFICE GANG FIGHT

The owner of a company had a daughter who was allowed to do whatever she wanted. He really had no idea what she was involved in after hours, and apparently she had become involved with a local tough gang.

One Friday afternoon, employees were still in the building and all was quiet. That was until loud motorcycles could be heard outside. The daughter looked nervous and told people to stay away from the windows. She also called the front desk and told them to not let anyone in. Well, a lot of good that did. The front desk person locked the doors and left the area in fear. Within minutes, guns were fired and everyone hit the floor in terror. The gang issued a few warning shots and then left the parking lot on their roaring motorbikes. Fortunately, the building was not struck by the bullets and no one was injured. They had aimed at the sky.

The daughter was escorted home by the police and was never seen in the office again. The owner was very embarrassed and forbade anyone to bring this up in the office. That was the end of the subject, however: the company had to find a new front desk person!

SHE'S LOOKING AT ME

This is a story about the kind of issue that drove me crazy in the business world. It's a story of two employees acting like sibling children. The contributor of this story related that these two employees were on the same team, although one was more experienced in how to do certain things than the other. For the sake of clarity, the employees will be called Sarah and Jane. Sarah was the more knowledge-able of the two.

Sarah was chatting with a coworker when Jane called to her from a few desks away with a work-related question, interrupting her conversation (later it was learned that it wasn't a work-related conversation). Sarah asked Jane to stop bothering her, and told her she would come by Jane's desk when she was done with her conversation. Jane took offense and left the office upset. She chose to work from her home the remainder of the day.

Someone got in touch with Jane and subsequently spoke with both women to learn more about what happened. It appeared that Sarah felt Jane was being rude by interrupting her when she was speaking with someone else, and Jane felt Sarah was being rude by continuing a casual conversation when a work question needed to be answered.

The following week, Jane sent Sarah an email requesting help with a work issue she was having. Sarah had not yet gotten to the email when Jane verbally asked her to respond so that she could complete the task. Sarah told her boss that Jane had raised her voice and that made her feel uncomfortable within the work environment.

The boss was working from home when this second incident occurred and asked them both to refrain from communicating with each other until she returned the following day. When she returned, both acknowledged that there was tension between them and both hoped it would be resolved. Jane felt bad; she did not want Sarah to feel uncomfortable, but she did not want her own work to suffer by not having the information to finish the assignment. Sarah felt that Jane's "behavior outbursts" were hostile and making it difficult to do her job. In a joint meeting, the boss let them both know that she would not tolerate any more of this behavior. Jane apologized to Sarah, but there was no reciprocal apology.

It continued. Jane sent an email to Sarah a few weeks later that Sarah felt was unprofessional and hostile. Sarah felt she was being "targeted" because their boss was copied in on the email. Evidently, a few days earlier, Sarah had made an error with a client and her boss had advised letting Jane know. Jane responded to Sarah's email (copying in the boss) to ensure she heard firsthand how Jane fixed the issue. This annoyed Sarah, but her boss told her to "Let it go."

The next week, they were back at it! Jane asked Sarah for some help with information so she could complete a task. Again, the boss was copied into the request. Sarah did not like that and responded to Jane using bold, red type. Jane took offense to the red type, but Sarah said she was simply trying to make it easy to spot her response. Jane asked Sarah not to use bold red font as she found it rude, unprofessional and insulting. The boss saw the exchange and wrote to them both asking to refrain from emailing each other!

Finally, Sarah sought help with HR and relayed all of the communication failures. She told HR that the breakdown in the relationship was affecting her personally and emotionally. HR met with the boss, who felt she had been taking appropriate action to get these two to work together more effectively. For whatever reason, they appeared to be oil and water and simply did not like each other, but the work must be done and this childish behavior must stop! No one was to blame, but they each needed to step back and consider their intent when communicating and see how the receiver perceived the message.

All was quiet for a few weeks and then it reared its head again. Sarah just wasn't going to let this thing go, and she wanted HR to know that she felt like the "victim" in the last meeting with HR, the boss, she and Jane. She felt "attacked." The HR person explained that no one was being attacked or blamed for these communications; the purpose of that meeting was to make both Sarah and Jane aware of their own feelings and how they perceived the other's motivations when engaging in email and verbal exchanges. It was not intended to upset either of them or have them feel defensive. When the meeting ended, it was felt that all involved had a clear understanding of the events that led them to that point and how they might move forward in a better place together.

Thirty days later, Sarah asked for an in-person meeting with HR. Sarah relayed that Jane had been staring at her from her desk. Jane had also used the copier closest to Sarah's desk and, while she was copying, was laughing to herself. Sarah was intimidated and chose to move to the conference room to work. She told HR that she was quite frustrated with the situation and also noted that she found it interesting that these events always came about when the boss was working from home.

The boss had requested that all email communications between Sarah and Jane went through her. Sarah felt like this had built a wall and prevented them from being able to address each other directly and work through their challenges. She finished by stating that she wanted permission to move to a conference room whenever she started to feel uncomfortable with her work environment.

HR then had conversations with Jane and the boss (separately). Jane felt that things had improved and were going well. She felt that there was finally a peaceful environment to work; she had taken all of the feedback seriously and was making a conscious effort to have better communications with all of her coworkers. Jane was stunned when she learned that Sarah was still feeling uncomfortable. She did not recall the "staring incident" or the "copier incident" and expressed that she needed her job and was doing everything she could not to put her job in jeopardy. She left quite shaken and sad.

The HR leader met with the legal department, they all felt that all of the concerns had been addressed. A summary of all that had transpired was created and given to both. They either needed to find a way to get along or it would be their choice to find work elsewhere. They were running a business not a day care or elementary school.

And that was the end of it. Or so it was thought ...

About a year later, Jane was reported to be an excellent worker and a very nice person but was showing signs of paranoia. Jane told someone in HR that she believed people were talking about her, even when she couldn't hear the conversations. She admitted that she hated to work alone, and when her paranoia erupted, she became very disruptive in the office. Jane also said that one day she had her head down working and when she looked up, she realized it was 5:55 p.m. and was alone in the office. She called her boss and left her a voicemail to say she was leaving.

In speaking with her boss, HR learned that the voicemail Jane left was quite scary. It sounded like she was traumatized or being held at knifepoint—it was very bizarre. The boss knew that Jane had had a very rough childhood in her home country and was very concerned about her.

Out of the blue one day, Jane asked her boss whether she needed to work from home because she smelled. Her boss said, "No! Did I say something to make you think that?"

Jane replied, "You didn't say anything."

Her boss took her into the conference room and talked with her. They agreed that no one had done or said anything about her dress or her smell. Her boss reinforced to her that she displays professionalism, she does not have an offensive odor and that her work is good.

She didn't stay with the company much longer.

RUMORED AFFAIR

HR received a call from an upset manager who reported he had been hearing rumors that HR was actively investigating an affair he was supposedly having with one of the sales leaders, an affair which, he said, was not happening. He was very upset that he had not been notified that he was under investigation.

The person in HR asked where/how he had received this information. He replied that he got a call from someone that used to be employed at this company, a guy he had never even heard of before! The HR person told him that there was no investigation that she was aware of. Perhaps he needed to confront the person who had contacted him and advise him that if he continued to talk about an affair, it would be considered slander (a spoken lie) and that he will not tolerate it. However, as a leader, if he was having a romantic relationship with a coworker, the policy was clear: it should be disclosed to ensure that the company was not seen to be colluding by paying for couples' expenses, travel, and so on.

He calmed down when he realized that this was some kind of hoax by someone who had an ax to grind with him or the sales manager. HR never knows what the next phone call will bring!

Keep your friends close and your enemies closer ...

CRAFTY COWORKERS

Jenny and Christine were coworkers who had a great working relationship in a retail store. Christine's husband was an artist who created art in various forms. Jenny was interested in buying something, and so Jenny and her partner met with Christine's husband and commissioned a piece to Jenny's specifications. A contract was signed and a money deposit was made.

When the piece was delivered, Jenny noted a few things she was not happy with and the changes were made. Each time a change was made and the piece was redelivered, Jenny came up with another item she was not happy with. After a few times, the craftsman advised Jenny that she was changing the original scope of the commission and any additional changes would require an extra charge. Jenny was not happy with this and shared her frustration. She wanted her money back.

The craftsman explained that he had met the obligations of the contract and that she owed him the rest of the money per the contract terms. This was really between the craftsman and Jenny.

Well, as you can imagine, Jenny brought her frustration into the store. This created quite a challenge for the office manager. Jenny was upset with Christine and was giving her the cold shoulder, even though Christine really had nothing to do with the transaction! They didn't want to be on the same shifts anymore. The situation was untenable and had to be dealt with.

The office manager made it clear that this situation was to stay outside of the store and the two had to find a way to work together professionally and to be respectful to each other. She needed them to act like adults because shifts and hours were not going to be changed just to suit them. If they couldn't get along, the store would no longer be their place of employment.

This is a great example of keeping personal situations out of the workplace—after all, managers are trying to run a business, not teaching children how to behave: That should have happened many years before!

SPURNED LOVER

HR got a call from an employee's fiancé demanding to know why the company was allowing a senior leader to have an affair with his bride-to-be. He sounded like he had been drinking, but one cannot jump to conclusions. The HR generalist asked a simple question: "Who are you talking about and how do you know this?"

The fiancé responded, "I know this because we were supposed to move to another state and she just told me she wasn't going because of this relationship with this guy (he named the person)." Now, of course, HR was on notice, so they had to check it out as she was a subordinate to him.

When HR called the female, she was very upset that her fiancé had brought her personal business into the office. What she does on her own time is not of concern to the company. She got quite belligerent and didn't want to talk about it. When HR let her know that the next call would be to the leader who her fiancé named, her entire demeanor changed. She preferred that he not be called, and stated again that she didn't believe what they did on their own time is of any concern to the company. Well, it was reported that she attended his team meeting and they stayed in the same hotel room on company time and the company expense report. As a leader, that went against policy. He would have to be called.

A call was made to the leader, and his response was that he "had done nothing ethically wrong from a company perspective." He did not believe that he had violated any leadership ethics. He said that they had only been flirting because they both had an attraction to each other, and he was certain that they intended to move forward with a relationship. He also apologized for putting the HR and legal team in that situation. He further stated his love for working in the company, and he hoped his performance would speak for itself, as if to say: *As long as I am performing my role, none of the policies really matter!*

HR received a call from the female. Her fiancé had been drinking a lot, which was uncommon for him. He was trying to get back at her for her indiscretions. He had not threatened her, but he said no one should be defending her after the way she had treated him. He said he was done calling people at her workplace because he knew the truth. The last comment he made was about the other guy and stated that, because he was short, "I could take him."

After a discussion with both of the couple's managers, legal, and HR, it was determined that while a policy had been broken in this consensual relationship, neither had denied the relationship and both had good performance records. However, they had used very poor judgment in front of their colleagues and put the company at a slight risk. They were reprimanded, and she was told not to travel with him on business. The relationship died its own death after that. They both escaped lightly and they knew it.

CONFERENCE ROOM MAYHEM

How much trouble can conference room scheduling cause? You might think not very much, but you'd be wrong!

This particular office had a centralized booking system for the conference rooms that were in constant use. The receptionist took her scheduling role very seriously; it was believed that she loved the power it gave her!

One day she was out getting supplies. When she returned, she found a "squatter" in a conference room that had been booked by someone else. This completely frustrated her because people were constantly taking conference rooms they had not booked, and she was left to do the explaining and had to get people to move. She walked into the conference room and asked the person if he was a participant in the meeting to be held next. He replied, "No," so she let him know that another person had booked the room. The occupant said, "Too bad, we are here now," and she felt brushed off and belittled.

"Fine," she said. "From now on, you can book your own conference rooms. I'm trying to do my job, and you are acting like a jerk!"

Well, she apparently said that to the wrong person. He went to his VP and demanded that she be terminated. In his words, "She flipped out!" The VP was dumbfounded. He knew there had been a problem, because she had just visited him, turned in her badge, and said she was done.

"What is going on?" the VP demanded. The "unauthorized" occupant of the conference room wanted her gone. He did not want to deal with her and her "control issues"!

The VP brought in HR to help sort this out because, within an hour of all this, she'd had a change of heart and did not want to quit her job. Through all of the subsequent conversations, it was learned that she felt disrespected all the time. People paid no attention to the "rules of engagement" for conference rooms. She constantly had to move people around and people would get annoyed with her, so she hated this part of her job. She had simply wanted to bring some order to the process without all the drama.

The VP in the office had no idea all this was going on or that she and the person she called a jerk were always butting heads. He tried to intimidate her. He liked using the conference rooms to conduct all of his business because he had a "cube" and not an office, even though that was not the correct use of the conference rooms.

The VP laid down the law, and the two of them were asked to call a truce. The VP told the male employee that future conference room requests had to go through the VP, who would provide the approval to the schedule administrator. This completely solved that issue of his abuse of the conference rooms and her having to get frustrated on a daily basis. However, it was an ineffective use of the VP's time.

An easy enough solution, but why can't people just get along?

Isn't it easier to be more collaborative rather than creating drama in the workplace? Put yourself in other's shoes and try to be kind to all you come in contact with. Help to create a great place to work!

WATER ATTACK

This happened at an event I attended.

A bunch of us were sitting around a beautiful fire pit at a luxury hotel enjoying a nightcap and some camaraderie. It was a perfect evening after a long day of meetings.

One employee, who does not drink alcohol, joined the group. For whatever reason, he put his fingers into his glass of water and started flicking water onto another employee who'd had a few drinks. Well, the "victim" totally flipped out! He jumped up, cursing worse than a sailor, and he was ready to take the guy out! I yelled to the two to stop it and to just calm down. The guy was out of control and could not contain his anger. The vulgarity coming out of his mouth was atrocious! I strongly encouraged him to let it go before he made a career ending mistake.

As I continued to try to calm him down, he shouted "NO! He knows I'm a germaphobe, and he is trying to antagonize me. He flicked water on me on purpose to get me angry!" I looked at the perpetrator and he simply shrugged his shoulders with a smile and walked away while the victim was still shouting at him. Children in adult bodies, I thought.

One of the other VPs in the group, calmly went up to the angry guy. He got him to call it a night and walked him all the way to his hotel room. The VP returned to the fire pit and let us know that he had done his good deed. I thanked him and said in jest, "I owe you for doing that, it could have continued to escalate."

He grabbed a cocktail napkin and jokingly asked me to put the IOU in writing, so I obliged and signed and dated it. That was the end of it until a few years later when the VP left the company. I received the napkin in a frame (see picture) from him with a note that said, "I am glad I didn't have to formally break the emergency glass, but thought I should give it back now."

I got a good laugh out of the framed note. I had no idea he actually kept the napkin all those years! I have blocked out the names for obvious reasons.

ARE YOU RECORDING?

There was an employee who was challenging to work with. The manager and coworkers walked on eggshells around her, concerned that no matter what they said or did around this employee, it would be misconstrued. She threw around the discrimination word a lot. She was highly skilled in her role and did good work, but she was challenged when it came to getting along well with others.

Finally, people around this person said they'd had enough, and a meeting was scheduled with her to get to the bottom of the issues. She came to the office with her cell phone. I saw her touch a button on the phone and place it near where I was sitting. After exchanging pleasantries, I asked, "Are you recording this conversation?"

To which she replied, "Yes."

I told her to turn the phone off because I did not give her permission to record our conversation and she did not give me a head's up that she would be recording. She complied, and I watched her turn the phone completely off. When I asked why she felt the need to secretly record the conversation, she said she wanted to "protect her rights." Quite frankly, I found it very gutsy to try to secretly record a member of the executive team!

I asked what rights she was protecting. I was simply there to learn more about her experience in her day-to-day work environment and help her have a better working relationship with colleagues. She replied that she wanted that, too. She wanted to come to work, do her job, and go home. She was tired of the drama that she had to deal with daily.

"What drama?" I asked.

"Every day it's something different. This person does or says this, I'm excluded from meetings, people seem to tiptoe around me, and it's ridiculous. I just want to do my job. I don't want friends—that's not why I'm here."

I asked what I could do to help her and she replied that she wanted people just to let her do her job and leave her alone. I responded that I would chat with her manager and work with both of them to create a space for her, if that is how she wanted it. I encouraged her to think about what team-work (one of the company values) looked like for her because the company was trying to create a work environment where people respected each other and didn't work in silos. Perhaps she might want to consider whether or not that was the work environment she wanted to be in going forward. Meanwhile, I would work with her to create space where she could do her best work. It was a good discussion, and she left, thanking me for listening and trying to help.

The manager and I worked together to create space, but she eventually voluntarily left the company. It was a learning experience for many. Just because someone appears hostile in a work environment, perhaps it's because they just want to be heard. Prior to that meeting there had been many conversations with the HR business partner, legal, and me in seeking ways to deal with this individual as negative interactions were common. There was a concern that she was trying to "build a case" as she made innuendoes to that effect constantly. Even the HR business partner wanted a witness to all conversations. We were certain that we had not heard the last of this person after she departed. While I am confident that she had been treated fairly, you just never know! She was never heard from again!

ALLEGED HR DISCRIMINATION

A member of the HR team at this company felt she was being singled out and discriminated against because of her race. One comment from a very inexperienced individual created a lot of team drama.

This person was fresh out of school and was in an entry-level position that required a lot of hands-on direction and training. She spoke with the HR generalist on the team that was also in the same office as she. He didn't know what to do because she was talking about his HR boss two levels up! He went to a senior HR generalist to ask what he should do.

Both decided to "investigate" without letting the leader know that this was going on. Protocol for investigations at this company was that when an employee brings up an issue regarding their manager, they are encouraged to speak with that manager first to solve it.

Evidently, in this instance, that protocol was not adhered to, and it appeared that the HR folks involved went on a witch-hunt to try to undermine the HR leader. The "lead investigator" assured members of the broader team that she had consulted with the leader, when in fact she had not. She tried to complete a covert investigation during an off-site full team meeting that was being facilitated by a highly respected outside individual. The facilitator picked up on the fact that something was going on in the room and brought it to light right there and then.

It is said that you could have heard a pin drop in that room when she stopped the session. She said, "Okay, I'm feeling a tension in the room, would anyone like to share what they are feeling?" Dead silence and eyes looking from one to the other as if to say, *I'm not talking, are you going to?*

Finally, someone found the courage and spoke up that a member of the team felt discriminated against and there was an investigation happening at breaks and lunch! The HR leader that was "under investigation" was shocked to learn about this in that manner. It took a lot of courage for one of the team members to speak up and disclose what was going on behind the scenes.

The facilitator took the learning opportunity and brought the elephant right into the room. It appeared that an innocent comment uttered to one person got blown out of proportion in the zeal of a "hot scoop." This turned into a full-blown team challenge that could have easily been avoided. The person who had uttered the innocent comment felt betrayed and did not trust her own team to listen to her and help her. She was embarrassed.

However, at the end of the session, the team was stronger, and all involved learned a hard lesson about operating within the HR team the same as you would operate if you were given this information for another team. In other words, do unto others as you do unto yourself!

HIRING & FIRING

LEADERSHIP CRAZINESS

This is a story that stretched over several years.

This organization had a leader who was a really nice person and an all right individual contributor but a terrible leader. Unfortunately, for quite a few employees, no one could or would make the decision to move this person along. The last year he was with the company created a lot of drama and havoc on the team both near and far.

The beginning of the end started with this person being unable to effectively deliver a performance improvement message to a team member. The HR team became frustrated and pointed out the pattern of ineffective communication with this person. The meeting to deliver the message to the employee was scheduled with HR invited to be on the call "for support." The HR person waited forty-five minutes before she sent a note asking if he had rescheduled the call—he replied he hadn't. He then called her back and stated that he delivered the message without her because "it just happened." He and the employee were going to set targets for him to work towards. This was counter to the plan that she and the leader had already decided and documented! What he sent her was a document that appeared to be a cut-and-paste from something else and not specific to this employee.

A few days later, the head of HR received a call about a confidential search going on to replace this leader. The head of HR expressed a concern over the impact that removing the leader would have on the target results he was accountable for in the business through his influence and expertise. The recruiter reported that she had no choice. For over six months, she had been receiving negative feedback on his performance and leadership. Time had been spent trying to find another role for him, but that did not appear to be coming to fruition, so it was time to start the confidential search. She advised the head of HR that the senior leader (who was in a different country) wanted to take away his management rights while they sorted through next steps.

Now, while that course of action may be normal in other parts of the world, it was not a practice in the United States. Here, if the person is not doing the job, you should either move him/her over or out. Once you start chipping away at their responsibilities, everyone knows what is going on and employees start to question the ability of the leadership to manage this person effectively. Not to mention the issue of paying them for a job they are not capable of doing.

A decision was made to talk with all direct reports of this leader to get a real pulse on what is happening within the unit. A total of seven individuals were spoken to, and the summary was that this leader was disorganized, changed direction constantly, did not have clarity of thought when giving direction, was not really familiar with the area he was responsible for, and he spent hours and hours creating internal work rather than focusing the team on the external environment and customer relationships. He appeared to be afraid of his direct manager, and when that manager said jump, his response was, "How high and which direction do you want me to face?" The entire team liked him as a person, but he was driving them crazy professionally. The confidence in the leadership was quite low within the team.

All of this was written up and reported back to the senior leader. His response? Make this go away! He did not have the time or energy to deal with it. As far as he was concerned, it was HR's area of expertise, and he expected HR to manage and deal with it. Complete and utter lack of accountability. Just pull out the checkbook and make this guy disappear! But because that's not how it is done, he stayed a while longer.

Another leader was asked to manage the "underperforming" employee on this team for sixty days. At the end of the sixty days, it was reported that his performance was not as bad as the inept leader had stated. The guy knew what he was doing, clients liked him, and he was on top of his projects … there must have been some mistake or misunderstanding! He further advised that there was nothing in this guy's performance that was so bad or critical that it warranted a performance plan. The HR leader knew what the problem was: The leader was in the wrong role and this poor employee was taking the fall for his boss's lack of skills and knowledge.

The bigger issue, however, was the strained relationship with this employee and others on the team. What to do? The recommendation was to let the leader go due to a lack of effective performance. Again, his boss wanted to buy him out and not deal with the poor performance issue. Because this action could have potentially set a precedent, HR advised against it, but ultimately, the business leaders make the decisions.

It took a few more months of drama before this leader was finally moved, along with a few others. The confidential search selection coincided with the lay-off. The poor performance was masked by a round of redundancies and, unfortunately, this person was never given appropriate feedback, so he would not get the opportunity to learn from the experience. In the end, the company simply moved the location of the role to a different country to avoid potential litigation.

More craziness...

A senior HR leader attended a local HR team meeting in one of the countries within her jurisdiction. The local HR manager presented a plan to start doing "top grading," which is a kind of interview process. About five minutes into his presentation, the senior global HR leader stood up and started ranting and raving, upset that every week she got requests from around the business to change this or change that without understanding how to implement things! She went on and on about too many teams trying to do their own thing, and she just couldn't have it.

The local HR manager was completely taken aback and disgusted. The sentiment was that the teams were not robots, and if the company wanted to treat them that way, the employees did not want to be a part of it. It was later learned that the team, after witnessing this outburst by a senior leader, started putting their resumes out, and during the course of the next year, there was a significant turnover from the manager role downward. The global HR leader had a long history of these outbursts in meetings and the behavior completely shut down the room. It was always considered that the global HR leader "had something on someone" given the many years of poor interpersonal behavior and turn-over on the team.

EXECUTIVE EAVESDROPPING

The executive team was in the middle of developing the following year's strategy. There was a lot that needed changing, and there were several new members on the executive team, so a decision was made to bring in a consultant to help think through some ideas to focus on for the coming year.

Whenever employees hear that the executives are working with a consultant, ears prick up and nerves get rattled. What will the consultant be doing? What's going on in those meetings? How am I or we going to be impacted? Rumors start flying, yet no one actually asks questions for reassurance.

As the planning progressed over the course of a few weeks, news was getting back to the executive team about what employees had been hearing … and it was 100 percent accurate! This was quite disturbing because nothing had been decided, and what was being communicated could be misinterpreted and damaging. Who was the mole on the executive team leaking information?

This company had a stellar IT leader, and it was decided that they would move to a "closed call" format that allowed the IT leader to see exactly how each person was dialing in either using an IP address or a phone line. This was not discussed with the broader team, only the CEO and head of IT knew it. The team was given new dial-in instructions and the call progressed, but not before the CEO asked the IT leader to do a quick check to see who was on the call.

He did this verbally so that individuals would not know that he was checking where the calls were coming from. Well, this little trick revealed there was an unidentified number. The CEO simply called the number and the person answered! When the CEO spoke, the call dropped. Ah ha! Caught!

The interesting thing about this is that the eavesdropper's boss thought that the individual was providing information to a top competitor only to learn that he was also a mole to the sales team as well. Needless to say, he was going to have to go dig his mole tunnels in another organization.

When asked, the mole said that he was so worried about losing his job if the company was reorganizing that he simply had to know what the executive team was thinking. Sadly, he was an excellent employee who would not have been impacted by any of the changes.

QBQ

At one company I worked for, I was involved in a plan to evolve the leadership development program (LDP). I visited the new learning and development leader at his office, and having never met in person before, we sat down to get to know each other. The first thing he did was to hand me a book.

He had simply walked into my office and said, "Denise, I wanted to share this book with you, I think you'll like it!" I read the title and subtitle and immediately started thinking he was sending me a message about myself. I looked at the book and asked him why he had given it to me.

He replied that he thought it would be a good book to add to the leadership development program. *Phew!* I then started laughing and shared with him what I was thinking when he handed me the book. He was apologetic and we both had a good laugh.

Well, after the first day of LDP, I received a phone call from the facilitator of the training that the new guy had not even read the book! He had hardly participated in the class discussion. The facilitator provided him the feedback that he was expected to participate, engage, and interact, but she got nothing back from him. She had even sent him the questions they would be using for the book discussion, but he had forgotten to take them with him to the session. He was generally disengaged. He stayed on his Blackberry (which tells you how long ago this was!) and remained in his seat during the breaks. This was the person that was to be the leader of LDP! It was also learned that he had not chosen the book, rather she had chosen it and the activity associated with it. He was just collecting a paycheck and adding no value.

As you can imagine, his term was quite short. Very interesting that he handed me a book about personal accountability, yet he had none.

Postscript: *QBQ* is an excellent book for anyone to read!

EXIT PACKAGE

There once was a salesperson who had been handed some lucrative accounts. As the economy changed, so did the buying habits on these accounts, and therefore, it was time for the salesperson to "hunt" for new accounts in order to meet his sales targets. It became obvious that he really didn't want to do that; he enjoyed making the "easy money."

A new sales leader came to town and started working with this guy in weekly meetings to brainstorm ideas on how to find clients, suggestions for who those clients might be, and so on. He kept asking for the sales leader to just reassign some accounts to him. Well, that was not going to happen. You "earn" commissions; you don't just sit back and collect commissions. After a few months, the heat was on and the sales guy was getting nervous. At the annual sales conference, he asked for time with the HR leader. They met in the lobby of the hotel, and he proceeded to describe his plight.

The salesperson said he was being treated unfairly. He always had this one account, but it was "taken" from him, and he was given other accounts to try to grow. This was a senior, experienced salesperson with close to thirty years' experience. He stated that he didn't want to start with new accounts. Would the company just give him a package and let him go? He was tired and simply didn't want to be at that company working for this new sales leader.

The HR leader explained that the company didn't have

"packages" to hand out. Further, it was suggested that he expend some of the energy in a positive way to grow his accounts. If he did that, rather than express his displeasure with his role and the expectations set for him, he would be successful and feel good about his accomplishments. He was told that asking an employee in a sales role to grow and sell into an account was the sales leader's basic role. The guy was nearly in tears, he wanted out but was not going to quit. He was given more encouragement to do what he knew best, which was to "sell into his account base" and to check back with the sales leader in the following month to see how far he'd come.

The following month he had made no progress with the accounts, and he was now being put on a performance plan. He wanted to chat with the HR leader again, as he strongly felt he was being mistreated. The HR leader took the call, gathered all of his input, and listened to him for a long period of time. Again, it was strongly suggested to follow the plan laid out, and he was told that he could and would overcome the performance plan. The company simply wanted him to get back to doing what they knew he could do, which was to sell and provide high quality client service.

The HR leader actually flew to his office and spoke with everyone to ensure that there was nothing unfair or illegal going on. People were open and that while some things were different from the prior leaders way of managing the team, they had no real complaints to report.

Unfortunately, he was never on board with the new assignments and sales requirements, and so he was reluctantly let go. As this was a performance termination, there was no severance package offered, but he promptly filed suit alleging age discrimination. If you read the "Rub and Tug" story, you'll know how the lawsuit process runs. For this case, the HR leader attended both depositions and mandatory arbitration. The sales leader was deposed and did a good job describing the expectations, the conversations, and everything that was done to get this sales guy to sell. He had simply "checked out" from his role and wanted out. At the time of his departure, he was earning base pay only (and had been for months because he had not earned commissions) and had no pipeline of clients or anything in his account base that might close in the foreseeable future.

Lawsuits take a long time to get to the deposition and arbitration phases. It was learned in the discovery process that the sales guy landed another sales role within four months of departing the company. However, he was let go from that company in less than a year for the same reason: no pipeline, no sales, and no proactivity to get there. This was very important to the defense of this case.

At the subsequent arbitration proceedings, after a full day of back and forth, the parties were very far apart and neither wanting to budge. In the interim, the former employee bought into a franchise that he knew nothing about and he was bleeding capital. This, along with the quick termination from the sales role, was also important to the case. Both parties were preparing for trial.

As these things go, there's a cost associated every time an attorney even thinks about a case. They wanted to try arbitration again. Finally, an agreement outside of trial took place, but he was still in the hole as the costs he had incurred with his attorney left him with far less than what the attorney earned, along with the several years of litigation that kept him focused on the lawsuit rather than finding ways to earn a living by following his passion. It was a very sad situation all around, as the company had been wrongly accused and had incurred defense costs, while the former employee wasted a lot of energy and money focused on being a victim of his own inaction, rather than feeding his soul and getting back to being the kind of top salesperson he had been all of his career.

I NEED AN ASSISTANT

An employee was putting together a complex deal. He advised that, in order for this deal to go through and be successful on the delivery side, he would need an assistant. There was no room for an assistant in the pricing of the deal, so he agreed to hire an assistant at his own cost just to get the deal done. It was left up to him, but there would be no funding from the deal for assistance.

After the deal was done and the delivery completed, soon thereafter a lawsuit came through referencing administrative help on the deal and the $15,000 billed for it. The employee was asked about it because it appeared he may have used his own company to charge the client as a subcontractor for this administrative help. When he was asked about it, he said he was not running his own business, but because his management team refused to fund this role for this deal, he was willing to "absorb the charges." He said that he had "worked a deal" with the client and built in the cost of the admin help; it was all "upfront in the paperwork." He had not hidden anything. He said the client was only interested in the total overall cost, not the administrative cost.

The employee then tried to say that he had worked with the internal contracts team to ensure that it was legitimate. He was very concerned that he may now lose his job over this. Evidently, what really happened is that the company was refusing to pay the unauthorized cost, and the subcontractor he had hired was now suing for nonpayment of services provided. He admitted that he knew he had no authority to do this, he also knew that the work would not have gotten done without this support. He was willing to pay the bill himself just to keep his job; however, he did not have the funds to pay it up front!

Digging a little deeper, it appeared that the employee added the cost to a fixed priced project and he was not forthright from the outset. Once he was told no, he tried to get it through anyway and submitted the cost for signature. Nevertheless, it was all somewhat hidden, and he knew it.

What his boss understood was that the employee was hiring the person on his own, knowing that it was not included in the price of the job and insisting that this person was his "personal assistant," not a part of the company. When his boss learned the truth and confronted him, the employee admitted that he lied but didn't know what else to do. He didn't feel like he could have delivered the work without this assistant. Another employee departed a company due to a poor decision.

PURPLE PROBE

This story is named for the car driven by the HR person in this particular company. Yes, she (let's call her Paula) drove a very purple Ford Probe, probably one of the ugliest and—in this case—the dirtiest cars anyone has ever driven or ridden in! It wasn't advisable to touch anything in that car. You might ask, "Why would someone even be in such a car?" The answer is that the employee offered to pick up her boss at the hotel and drive him to a meeting about an hour or so away. The boss was shocked when this ugly, dirty car pulled up and wondered who would offer a ride and not clean out the car? Anyway, that is not the real story here...

Paula's Purple Probe became legendary. Even the boss's kids knew about it and its driver. She was a very attractive person, whose behavior was so inappropriate that it was clear human resources was not the career she was best suited for. Everyone knew it, but no one told the HR leader what was really going on, perhaps because they found "The Purple Probe" so entertaining and didn't want the fun to end.

But when she finally left the company, the stories came out. The first real hint that something was not quite right was when the HR leader learned that the Christmas office party game was to be adult Twister. When contacted, Purple Probe replied, "I thought it would be better than just standing around drinking and talking. It could get people engaged and laughing." To which the leader replied, "Oh, I'm sure

it would, and that is not all it would accomplish! As an HR professional, how could you think that this game would be an appropriate workplace activity? Did you consider the potential legal exposure for hostile work environment? Did you think that people touching each other while drinking alcohol was a good idea?" Purple Probe said she hadn't thought of that. Good grief, *really?*

As the stories continued to come in, the HR leader was amazed. At an office happy-hour event, it was reported that Purple Probe and a married male employee were seen kissing. It was general office knowledge that they were in a relationship. The feeling was that she was pursuing him and he was a willing participant. Some of the women and a number of the men in the office described her flirtatiousness around men. They felt Purple Probe used her body to attract attention, especially with the type of clothing she wore, which were more suitable for a nightclub than the office. She appeared to love to bounce around the office swinging her beautiful locks around along to attract attention. On the other hand, the male referred to her touching as "casual contact," but they did not find it offensive. One male employee even went so far as to state that he felt embarrassed for her because she was the brunt of many jokes and innuendo around the water cooler. Another guy explained that she pursued him when he first started the job, asking personal questions, touching his arm, and so forth. He became concerned that people were getting the wrong message. She often wanted to go out with people socially after hours, especially the guys in the office. Paula was normally the one to suggest a happy hour, and it could be any day of the week, not the normal Friday afternoon happy hours.

Employees did not trust her and would not seek her

out for help if they needed something. Instead, they stated that they had to "go around her" to get their HR questions handled. On occasion, she evidently also shared a company paid-for condo with a male sales leader who lived in another country. When he came to the US, they would sometimes hook up. In one instance, the senior sales leader for that office walked into the man's office without knocking and found the two kissing, and several other employees saw it too. The senior sales leader said that he saw it as a "momentary lapse in judgment" and let it go! This story also did not come out until she was long gone.

The amazing part of this story is how long fellow employees allowed serious transgressions to continue without stepping up to protect the company. But, even more amazing was the phone call the HR leader received from one of the office managers where Purple Probe worked. He said that Paula did a lot of good things for some people, and the office was upset that she was dismissed. He even went so far as to say that there was a "lynch-mob mentality" against those who had reported her behaviors. He had received questions from nine different people (the HR leader was ready to bet they were all male) wanting to know why she was removed from the business. The HR leader related to him that termination decisions are never taken lightly and that all he needed to know was there had been just cause.

Remarkably, this was not the last the company saw of Paula. The next time Purple Probe was seen by employees was in a magazine photo advertising hair products! She did have beautiful hair.

DOUBLE DUTY

Sometimes, one job is not enough and many people have to work two jobs. But how is it possible to work two jobs simultaneously and get paid for being in two places at once, unbeknownst to both employers? It's not as unlikely as it sounds.

Side Work

In the case of one employee, there was an agreement that he could pursue work outside the company on the condition that the other work did not interfere with his existing work commitments and that extra work was with an organization that was not a competitor.

A year later, this employee submitted a time card for sixty hours of work. It included hours for a client that the company did not do work for, which prompted an investigation that disclosed he missed a mandatory training and a conference, even though the company had paid for his attendance.

Of course, the manager brought him in for a chat. The manager advised that he needed evidence that the employee had actually worked those sixty hours before he could approve the timecard, but he resigned on the spot and said, "Just forget about it, I'm done."

Here and There

In another example, HR received a call from a former employee who wanted the company to know that one of its current full-time employees was also working full-time at a competitor's company. Apparently, the caller went on to state that a particular manager at the company was aware of this situation and was letting it go on.

HR contacted the manager and learned that he did indeed know, but he had raised the issue with the direct manager of the individual concerned. A further call revealed that the manager had chatted with the employee, who had denied it, so the matter had stopped there!

Obviously, that was not good enough. HR called the other company to talk with its HR department, confidentially, but the entire HR team was out for the remainder of the week at a conference. While on the call, however, HR gave the name of the two-timing employee and asked the operator if the man was in the company's phone directory: Affirmative! When HR contacted the man's manager at the other company, a "bad connection" led to the call being disconnected, and it was impossible to get the manager back on the line. Another person agreed to connect HR with the manager, but there was no response. Nothing.

Later that day, HR called the company again and obtained some additional information, specifically that the employee had been at the new company for two weeks. After consulting with the legal department and senior leadership, immediate termination was completed and payroll was stopped.

Obviously, many people work more than one job, a practice known as moonlighting. However, working at two places during the same work hours, when you can't be in two places at one time, is a form of theft if you are on the payroll as an employee. In addition, if you are in a sales role, working at two competing companies at the same time, you have access to confidential company information that could be used to win a competitive bid—totally unethical. This is always a terminable offense, and I caution anyone who's considering moonlighting that you will always be discovered; it's just a matter of time!

I WANT TO BE A VP!

After the usual small talk, the following career discussion took place between an employee and an HR leader.

Employee: I want to be a vice president. I'm ready.

HR leader: Okay, a VP of what?

Employee: I don't know, but all my friends are VPs, and I think I have shown my talents, so I deserve to be a VP.

HR leader: I appreciate that you want to be a VP; we all want to move up the ladder. However, that being said, it doesn't work that way. First, there has to be a business need for a VP role, the role is funded and advertised, then interviews are completed and a selection made based on knowledge, skills and abilities.

Employee: I understand that, so I have put together a business plan for a VP role that I believe I'm the best candidate for.

HR leader: Thank you for taking the initiative to do this. I'll certainly review it from a business perspective and get back to you.

Employee: Thank you so much, but this is my job. I need to be named a VP!

HR leader: And what will you do if this role is not feasible in the business right now?

Employee: I'll keep pushing and doing my job as I always have, but I want you to know that my goal is to be a VP in the very near future. I really don't want to leave the business, but this is very important to me.

HR leader: Thanks for coming in. I commit to reviewing the proposal and talking to the decision-makers. You are a valued employee, and we don't want to lose you, but we cannot create jobs or job titles for everyone that wants a new role or title. It's dictated by the needs of the business. Keep up the good work and let's chat again in the next month.

This story is included to show that it's not always drama that HR deals with; sometimes, they are called upon to set employee thinking on the right track. A little advice for employees is to focus on the role and value you bring to an organization and not the title.

QUICK EXITS

One would think that new employees would be on their best behavior the first few weeks, but not so for some! These stories are truly deserving of my signature comment: Good grief!

Rude and Crude

This has to go down as one of the shortest tenures of any employee I've ever known. Be warned: This story is R rated, and it goes like this...

An employee was hired to work with customers and, after the normal onboarding process, she was flown to her first client meeting. One of her male colleagues picked her up from the airport and they talked about the client meeting they were heading to. She started right in with quite inappropriate comments about what had happened with the client thus far and dropped the F-bomb several times en route to the meeting. Her colleague was taken aback by the comments and language—after all, he had been on the woman's interview team!

Later that evening there was a client dinner. Her drink of choice was a Lemon Drop (a mixture of vodka, triple sec, simple syrup, and fresh lemon juice). In the course of the evening, she commented to one of her other male colleagues that he could refer to her as a "bitch" if he was pulling her hair or grabbing her ass. Unfortunately, subordinates at the table heard this.

Noticing that a colleague was quite uncomfortable, another coworker recommended that she listen more and talk less. Apparently, that was not the game plan. The next thing she said was that it is quite okay for the guys to send her "hard penis shots." The team did their best to distract the client whenever she started to talk!

They weren't too successful with that. Before anyone could stop her, she told one of the client representatives that her company was "fucked up, disorganized, and ill prepared." Sadly, it did not end there. Among her other indiscretions, she talked about being "a hot mess" on Sunday morning, she called a colleague "an amateur," asked someone if her tits looked big, and made several dick-sucking and pussy-eating references. Needless to say, some at the dinner lost their appetites.

The team had additional challenging meetings with this individual, but nothing as blatantly unprofessional as that dinner meeting with the client. Furthermore, back in the office, she was constantly throwing members of the team under the bus.

As the interactions escalated, the team leader decided to ask for her "side of the story" and learned from her that she believed the team was not performing the way the client needed or wanted. She saw her interactions with the client as "normal camaraderie building" and that she "had the client in the palm of her hand."

At this point, the client team was at a loss about how they could continue working with her. This person clearly was not representative of the company's values and mission, and so the decision was made to terminate her employment before it got any crazier. Ten days after she started work, she was back on the market looking for another opportunity, and not a moment too soon for the client team.

Missing Person

An individual was hired to work at a client's site. There was a weekend project cutover scheduled for his first job, and he was a no show. Nobody could find the guy, and he didn't respond to calls or emails. He was finally located late Sunday evening and said he was staying at a Travelodge in the city where he lived. He said he was in an accident on Saturday and could not work on Sunday, and he added that his cell phone was stolen. Talk about unlucky!

But things started sounding a little fishy. HR was asked to send a local employee over to the Travelodge to investigate what was going on, but the employee reported that no one by his name was registered there. This mystery was never resolved because the individual was never heard from again! He simply vanished into thin air, and HR had to send a termination letter to his last known address.

Where Are You?

A new member of staff was hired to work with a specific client. The client introduction was to take place at 10:00 a.m., but the newbie was nowhere to be seen. A quick call to her revealed that she believed the meeting was to be at 11:30 a.m. "No," replied her colleague, "the meeting was at ten. Where are you?"

"I don't own a car, so I'm at the car rental place, but I

have credit issues and they are giving me a hard time about renting the car. Can you pick me up and bring me back?"

Well, there was no way they were going to make the client meeting now. The tenured employee made the appropriate excuses to the client and then let the manager know.

Of course, a call to HR was in order! HR advised the manager to talk with the new hire and ask her if she had transportation to get to and from the job site? If the answer was no, it would be necessary to let the person go. Employees must be able to fulfill the minimum requirements of the role, which in this case involved getting to the job site!

MISCALCULATION

If you ever decide to leave a company, it's very important to know all the policies before quitting, especially as it relates to getting paid leave, bonus calculations, final pay, and so on. This is a story of one person who didn't, and it did not turn out so well for him.

A business leader at a company was on an annual bonus plan that included a policy clause defining how and when the bonus was earned and paid. As a leader, he was held accountable for not only knowing the policy for himself but also to be able to articulate it to his direct employees. In other words, he was held to a higher level of accountability on this topic than other employees. The policy clearly stated that one must be employed at the time the bonus was paid, which means that if you were to leave prior to the bonus payment date, no payment would be forthcoming.

The business leader voluntarily resigned and left the same day as he gave notice. The date of notice and departure was exactly two weeks prior to bonus payments being made. The employee went to work for a competitor, starting work on the same day as the notice.

When the bonus payment date came and went without money hitting his account, he sent an email to the HR team. A response was put together with copies of the policy, explaining that the nature of his resignation and departure meant he was ineligible for the bonus. He filed a claim with his state's labor board.

In an attempt to save the company legal costs, an offer of 10 percent of the disputed payment was made to the former employee. He declined the offer and pushed for a hearing with the administrative law judge of his state. Unfortunately for the company, the former employee resided and worked in California, one of the most employee-favorable states in the United States.

The HR leader flew to the hearing, represented by counsel. The employee represented himself at the hearing. The judge took testimony from the HR leader and the former employee. She reviewed all of the documents as well as the testimony and found in favor of the company. It seems that since the employee was a manager at the company it was expected that he would know the policies. He needed to only wait two weeks to get his money before he departed. He could even have given two weeks' notice and would have still been eligible for payment! No appeal was ever filed. He should have taken the token offer ...

SHE'S TOO SEXY

An office needed a new HR leader, and so the search began. But it proved to be a challenge. One candidate didn't have enough experience with certain things, one seemed to have an attitude, one had never worked in the industry, one couldn't answer all the questions, another one seemed too shy, and the list went on. The candidates who were interviewed were simply not a good fit. This company also had the complexity of a union to deal with, which is never easy for the HR team or the company.

Finally, a seemingly excellent candidate appeared in the mix—at least she was good on paper. Her experience was exactly what the team had been looking for: great tenure in the field, good union experience, and her education background was top-notch. The candidate had even worked in the same industry! The panel agreed that the person had aced the interview, yet they were still hesitant to move forward.

Despite having all of the credentials, one of the males on the interview panel actually stated that she was too attractive for the role and she was too upper class! He was concerned that the union would not relate well to this person, especially the union leaders. The business leader could not believe his ears. A lot of discussion ensued.

Finally, the team wore the guy down, and the right decision (or so it seemed) was made to hire the woman for the knowledge, skills, and abilities she brought to the role.

This entire process took nearly four months to complete. Thankfully, the feedback from all involved with her was that, seven months into the job, it was the best hiring decision ever made. Who would have imagined that all that went on behind the scenes of a simple hiring?

Fast forward two years, it became evident that the first impression was accurate, she was not a good fit and she was asked to leave the organization, but not before leaving some damage in her wake. We've all heard the "first impression, lasting impression"; well, it appears to be true in this instance.

BLATANT LIES

Certain businesses rely on staff having technical certifications, just as a teacher needs a teaching credential, attorneys must pass the bar, and CPAs must pass the CPA exam. One such certification in the technology world is a PMP, Project Management Professional. When contracting with clients, they will pay a higher hourly rate for a PMP than for a non-PMP. In addition, some vendors require an organization to have a certain number of certified professionals on staff. For example, suppliers often offer discounts based on a company's total number of PMP certifications. These are industry best practices.

Organizations rely on employees being honest about their certifications. Usually, employees must produce their certificate, but in one instance, that requirement slipped through the cracks, and the organization relied on the employees' word. During a routine audit of the files, it was noted that an employee had stated in his application that he held a PMP certification. It was put into the system and the data was given to one of the vendor partners to attain a higher level partner agreement.

The employee was asked to produce the documentation, and he said he would. Time went by and nothing was produced. So the HR person took matters into her own hands and called the PMP Institute and learned that they had no record of this person's certification. She pushed the employee hard to confirm his certification. He promised to get it: there must be a mix-up at the institute! Finally, after the third push from HR, he said he would resign because he couldn't supply the proof. Would you believe that the manager said he would have "to think about it" when the employee tendered his resignation?

The manager told HR that while the employee had lied about his certification, there were two large projects coming up that he was involved in and they needed his help with. If they were to fire him now, the projects could be in jeopardy. The manager said he needed time to figure out a transition plan. HR asked him what he was planning to tell the client, which seemed to bring the manager back to his senses.

Termination occurred that afternoon because the manager finally realized that he could not perpetuate the lie with the client. He understood that it would be better to be up-front and jointly come to an agreement with the client about the project timeline rather than keep the secret. Sometimes panic mode does not allow for clear thinking. Why would someone lie about such a thing and jeopardize their integrity and reputation?

COLLEGE DEGREE?

Sometimes, job candidates can really keep the recruiter, hiring manager, and others involved in the process on their toes. The incident described in this story happened more times than I have fingers and toes to count them on, so it is worth writing about. Each time it happened, I found myself saying, "Good grief! I'm sure life does not have to be so complicated!"

Countless candidates get all the way to the offer-of-employment stage and still think they can pull a fast one. I'm sure that some might even get away with lying on their application, but is the risk really worth taking?

One particular time, a female was made an offer contingent upon successfully completing the background check. The company looked at criminal, education, and DMV records to verify what was on the application matched reality. (As an aside, the reason that companies have you complete an actual application and won't just accept a resume, is that the application contains the legal language similar to "I affirm that all information contained in this application is true and correct," which is similar to taking an oath in court.

The candidate indicated that she had received a college degree from a certain school. The school reported that she did not receive the diploma nor had she actually graduated. When asked about this, she hedged and stated she had earned the degree because she had completed all the coursework. HR went back to the school, as there was a chance that the school had made a mistake. The candidate had insisted that she was a graduate of this college.

The school advised HR that she had charges for an unreturned library book that she had not paid! They had withheld her diploma for this reason, so she was listed as not graduating. When asked about this, she admitted she was aware of the school's punitive action and that she didn't have (or would be getting) a diploma from this institution. Well, why didn't she just say that in the first place? The role, while at a senior level, did not actually require a degree, but it did require integrity. The offer was rescinded for failing to disclose what she already knew to be true when asked. A very sad situation that could have been avoided; she expressed astonishment that the company took that stance.

And another one …

A background check from the school listed by a potential new hire indicated he had "no record of attendance." HR called the candidate and he reassured them that he had a degree that was obtained through the army.

HR asked him to send a copy to be reviewed. He said the original was with the Veterans Administration and he would get a copy. A few days letter, HR received a copy of a letter confirming the degree, however the college name in the letter was misspelled. Somewhat confused, HR contacted the VA again. The VA advised HR that the letter had been altered, so the company made another request for the original from the applicant. After letting the candidate know what had happened, he withdrew his name from selection and stated he did not want to pursue employment any longer. Clearly he had attempted to pull the wool over HR's eyes, probably because the job being offered would have given him a substantial salary increase compared to what he was earning at his current employer.

And finally...

A guy was hired to lead a team, but he sent the HR team on a wild goose chase trying to verify his degree. He finally admitted that while he attended the school, he actually obtained his degree document from an individual that sells forged documents on the internet. You name the school and he produces the fake degree for you to give to the employer! The problem, however, was that most employers check with the institution! He was advised that the next time he sought employment, he should leave the degree off because lying never pays. He was asked to move on.

UNDERSTANDING HEALTHCARE

An employee of this company came from prior employment at Microsoft. He was very intelligent and in high demand for his top skills in IT. He was so busy that he never really took the time to understand medical coverage and how it works in the United States. As with many large companies like Microsoft, they have comprehensive policies with a very low copay, and almost everything is covered 100 percent after the copay. That is not true for most companies these days. This particular individual had previously worked outside of the United States and worked for the "big boys" most of his career.

The challenge was that this employee's spouse had some medical issues to be handled. He hadn't realized that, after the copay, he was also subject to an annual deductible. Certain things, at the time, were also not covered. This employee went crazy and went on an email writing campaign and tried to drop every name he could think of to get someone to change what was covered and what his out-of-pocket should be. His phone conversations with the HR benefits person were rude and condescending. He was a very well compensated employee (earning a high six-figure salary), but aren't they the ones that shout the loudest? Anyway, he didn't understand his policy and didn't have time to understand it.

Finally, he demanded that someone from the benefits team fly across the country to meet with him and his wife and go through everything with them. The HR benefits person complied as she needed to put a stop to the emails and phone calls! The benefits representative spent seven hours at the employee's dining room table going through every single question, bill, and concern that he and his wife had. It didn't change the outcome from a dollar perspective, but he certainly learned a lot and learned that he needed to be accountable for knowing his plan and how to maximize his benefits. He was still very upset and very vocal that someone at his level was not being given preferential treatment. He didn't get that this company had a benefits plan that did not discriminate based on hierarchy.

He then spent the next few months trying to lobby the company to get into the "same league as the big boys in tech" as it relates to medical benefits. Finally, he realized that what he wanted was not going to happen at this low-margin company and he moved on. The benefits person who spent seven hours with this guy, not counting the many hours on phone and email, was not sorry to learn of his departure.

LOVE TRIANGLE

It is challenging to have an office romance, especially when it sours. It is even worse when it sours and one of the employees picks up with a third employee! To further complicate this particular situation, the first male of the couple involved was the son of a leader in the organization!

A guy and a gal were in a relationship. This was not a one-night stand but an actual relationship that looked like it was going in the right direction—until it ended. The guy was also having employment performance problems and had been put on performance improvement notice. His manager was delicately trying to work through it, crossing all the T's and dotting the I's in deference to this guy's well respected father who was in the business.

The gal then started a relationship with another guy in the business, a supervisor. The first boyfriend began visiting her Facebook page and making comments as well as visiting the new boyfriend's Facebook page. She started getting frustrated and annoyed with him. She spoke with him about his behavior, but he denied doing anything wrong.

Next he started following the two of them around and just "happened" to be at the same restaurants, stores, and other places they were. He denied that it was him in the car they reported seeing. "Just coincidence," he said. The woman started to freak out and went to HR when she began receiving emails from his office email address.

He got called in by HR, and he claimed that someone must have gained access to his system—after all, the company was full of IT people. He denied following the new boyfriend and told HR he had never even met him. Well, that was definitely a lie as they had, at one time, worked on the same project!

HR asked him to bring in his laptop and IT would take a look at it. He complied but his laptop had been completely wiped clean. HR wondered how that had happened! During many conversations with him, he maintained denial. It was finally decided that, since he was responsible for the laptop and it had been wiped, he had violated IT policy. He had been blatantly lying to HR, and his performance was not improving matters, so it was clear he had to be sent on his way.

Prior to letting him go, a conversation was had with his father as a courtesy. He was not surprised and promised to do what he could to help his son move on. That was the end of the story, but it appears that losing his job was the wake-up call he needed, which the source of this story was relieved to hear. He finally stopped bothering his ex-girlfriend and life went on.

NOT THE PERFECT CANDIDATE

An employee had just received word from a manager that he was being promoted to a new role. He was very excited until his manager made a comment: "You are not the perfect candidate, but we are going to offer it to you." He was really expecting to hear, "Congratulations, you've been selected!" Needless to say he was quite disappointed and called HR because he wasn't sure he wanted to continue to work under this manager, even if he had been promoted.

The history ran pretty deep with these two. There were already communication challenges. On one occasion, at an event, the manager appeared to have had too much to drink and asked the employee to meet him outside. He complied. On the way outside, the manager stopped at the bathroom and asked the employee to come with him. He refused because he was holding a glass of wine. When they finally got outside, the manager took the glass of wine and smashed it against the wall. Some of the hotel people saw it and ran over to clean it up.

There was a Starbucks in the hotel lobby, so the employee took the manager to the coffee shop and spent an hour with him before finally leading him to his room. During their time in the coffee shop, the manager ranted and raved about everyone he disagreed with and the people he thought were incompetent: No one was safe from being thrown under the bus. The employee was quite concerned about taking on more responsibility and accountability for someone who was so opinionated and disrespectful. However, despite this history, the man took the promotion.

He didn't last long because the manager continued his antics. He made it challenging for the newly promoted employee to do his best work. There was also another employee who reportedly applied to get out from under this guy.

The saying goes, you only get to pick your boss once—when you are offered a position and you say yes. After that, the company can move managers around and you then have to decide if you want to stay with that manager or not. This guy chose not.

Author's note: Your first reaction or gut is probably what you should follow. This person should have gone with his gut and not taken that job!

CONSIDERING RETIREMENT

This company had two layers of HR leadership. One ran the global level and one ran the local, regional level. The local HR leader was *considering* early retirement and, as a courtesy, had a conversation with the global leader to let the company know what she was thinking. The global leader was appreciative of the heads up.

A few months later, another conversation was had and the global leader advised the regional leader that he was going to begin the search for her replacement soon. The regional leader was surprised and advised the global leader that, under the terms of the employment agreement, the regional leader was required to give sixty days written notice, which she had not yet done. She promised she would provide that at the appropriate time based on when she planned to leave.

The global HR leader's facial expression completely changed, and he became quite angry. He stated that based on the prior conversation, he had given his boss notice of the regional leader's plan to leave and had been "working towards that." He stated that it was too late to change because he could not go back to his boss and tell him that he was incorrect and spoke prematurely!

The regional HR leader was astounded. What was this person getting so angry about? The global leader needed to understand that, since there had not been the required notice, there was no formal resignation. Therefore, if the global HR leader didn't want the regional person to stay, a sixty-day written notice of termination would need to be given. The global head of HR was livid. He said he would "take this under advisement" and get back to her with what the company wanted to have happen!

A few weeks later, another conversation between these two took place. The global head of HR had a completely different demeanor. He stated that he understood what had happened, he wanted the regional HR leader to send a note to his boss stating that she was "recanting the conversation" about leaving. The regional leader said that she was happy to write to his boss, but she would not use those words. The regional leader also let the global leader know how surprised she was at the global leader's reaction during the conversation a few weeks back. The regional leader thought that the global leader would be relieved that she was staying, given how complimentary of her work he had always been.

The global leader simply said that he always thought when the CEO left at the end of the year, that the regional leader would go as well, as that had been part of several conversations. He said he would let his boss know that the regional leader was staying and that he "would let the new CEO know about both conversations and let the new person decide."

The regional leader asked, "Decide what?"

The global leader said, "Whether or not they want you on the team."

The regional leader thought that was quite interesting and became quite angry and frustrated. She ended up staying three more years but still had to deal with the lunacy of the global HR leader throughout that time.

NEW-HIRE ANTICS

How can one person create so much drama in the first week? That was the question the supervisor asked the HR business partner one day. Patience was already thin, and the female employee had only been there for five work days!

On day two, a coworker notified the supervisor that the new employee had spent most of the day on the phone. She was not doing any of the assignments given to her and had not even turned on her computer. The supervisor chatted with the new employee and her response was that as soon as she had some real work to do there would be no more phone calls during the day! "Okay," said the supervisor, "let me be clear. Here are the things you need to do every day, let's get started now. I need you to get off on the right foot with us."

On day three, the new employee showed up in flip-flops. Another conversation with the supervisor resulted in the response: "I thought it was a trade-off because it is really hot in here." *Oh my*, thought the supervisor, *there is definitely a lack of business acumen with this one.*

What would day four bring? Well, she must have had a reading comprehension issue because she showed up in an athletics track suit. She had received the dress code on the first day, she had had a conversation about flip-flops on day three, and now a track suit? This employee really knew how to push the limits. Another conversation with the supervisor made it clear what the dress code "rules" were in that office, actually reading the code out loud to her. "Any questions?" the supervisor asked. "No, I've got it, thanks," she said.

Just when you think it couldn't get any worse, it did! The team went to lunch and she made a few sexual innuendos at the table. It was also noted that she often left her desk to visit one of the male coworkers. Finally, she was asked by a coworker: "Do you like it here?" She replied, "Yes, everyone is very nice, although the women are quite 'clique-y.' Two of the ladies are very quiet and stay to themselves. I sense some tension between some of the folks, and I've been called into the supervisor's office twice already. I am starting to feel like I am being victimized. It's been really hard to slip in and be a part of the team. One person greets everyone but says nothing to me, and on the third day she actually gave me a look that could kill."

The coworker responded that in her opinion, the new employee appeared to be more interested in the guys, one in particular, than in making friends with the other female teammates. She told her that she had been seen putting her arm around his shoulder and talking loudly. She had also been heard saying to him, "I'm going to be alone this weekend. What are doing this weekend?" The coworker told the new employee that the male employee was starting to feel uncomfortable around her. She knew this because she had seen him make the "she's crazy" sign with a circular finger motion beside his head whenever the new employee turned away from him.

She further told the new employee that many of her comments, in her opinion, had sexual overtones and were inappropriate in the workplace. "That's not how this office operates," she'd told her, "and if you want to be successful here, you may want to rethink how you interact with people in the office."

The next day, day seven, the coworker received a call from the new employee saying, "I'll miss you, and thanks for talking with me." She had just been fired and said she was angry and upset. The now ex-employee said she believed the supervisor had it in for her from the beginning. But she told the coworker not to worry about her because she had a lot going for her and would be just fine. That was the last the coworker ever heard from that person.

It just goes to show that you just never know from interviews how a person will show up to do their job and fit in.

ODDS & ENDS

HYGIENE

These stories can be a little disgusting, but they still need to be told.

Ladies' Room

The HR leader took a call from another office from an employee at the end of her rope. She was sick and tired of the restroom challenges in a small, mostly female office. She had put up signs asking people to clean up after themselves, she had made "loud comments" when she entered the restroom and found a mess, and she had even asked someone who sat near the bathroom to monitor who went in and came out, but nothing was working! Somehow, there was always a mess when she entered the bathroom! It was her opinion that, as an employee, she should be able to expect to have access to a clean bathroom during work hours. She basically begged the HR leader to visit the office. Plans were made for the HR leader to go to the office (a flight away) and meet with the women. After all, this bathroom was only used by that company's employees!

The meeting was scheduled without a subject and employees were told to just be there! The HR leader had a very frank discussion with the employees about flushing the toilet after use, taking care of their personal hygiene items, picking up whatever they drop on the floor before they leave, using the air freshener when appropriate. She told them that bathroom wipes were provided for a reason! As the National Parks request of visitors, the women were asked to "leave no trace." They were all quite embarrassed and shocked that the head of HR had to fly to their office to have this discussion. There was never another complaint about the bathroom facilities at that office.

Men's Room

The business had recently moved into an office building that shared the restrooms with another business. After a few months, the facilities person started getting complaints from the landlord that since her company had moved in, there had been "issues" with the men's bathroom. Someone was using the stall instead of the urinal and in doing so, he was hitting the seat and urine was on the floor. The facilities manager would notify the office of the problem, and she also asked the landlord to post signs to help get the message across.

Not long after, another call from the landlord came in. The situation is getting worse. The other tenant was getting quite frustrated and angry. In fact, one of its male employees has stated that it was definitely one of the other company's employees to blame. He had been using a stall one day when the person in the next stall had "sprayed" him. It was just one man's word against the other: no photos, no proof. The facilities manager asked for a description of the person and the landlord promised to get one.

In came another call from the landlord, who had been given a detailed description of the offender by an employee of the other tenant, who knew exactly what the person was wearing. The victim said that after his shoe had been sprayed with urine, he followed the guy to the office suite of his company. With the description in mind, the facilities manager walked around and spotted the offender ... the person was on the HR team! *Oh my, you have to be kidding me!* she thought, and she referred the problem to the HR leader.

The HR leader met with the alleged culprit, who profusely denied being the problem. The HR leader had little choice but to make him aware that this challenge existed and hope he would stop. So she took him at his word and sent him back to work.

But the next week, the phantom urinator was back. This time, the neighboring office worker took a photo of the employee leaving the bathroom. It was the same guy! The facilities manager got yet another phone call and then made a follow-up call to the HR leader. She was quite frustrated. In the second conversation with the male employee, she disclosed that he had been photographed leaving the bathroom after a mess was left. Even then, he still denied it, but she gave him a stern warning that he needed to be careful, practice good hygiene, and leave the bathroom neat and tidy.

Thankfully, there was never another complaint, and HR was relieved to know the challenge was resolved.

Body Odor

Two members of the staff approached their manager to complain about a female colleague's body odor. They had had enough and wanted their desk moved. Her body odor was repulsive, they said. "How could she not know? She's dating someone, she has children! We do not want to be near her, and we do not want to be the ones to tell her. You must do something."

Well, thought the manager, *this is not going to be easy.*

To make matters worse, the woman was her sister-in-law's cousin! What was the best way to handle this delicately? Should she simply put a deodorant stick on her desk? The manager spoke with several colleagues and then went to HR for advice about the best way to handle such a delicate topic.

HR gave great advice. "Have a gentle, direct, information chat," the HR leader said. "She may not even be aware."

"Are you kidding?" said the manager. "I can't do that!"

"Yes, you can," the HR leader replied.

The manager fretted over this for several days. The more she thought about it, the worse it got. Meanwhile, the two employees became more frustrated. "When are you going to fix this?" they asked.

No time like the present, thought the manager. Knowing she couldn't put it off any longer, she asked the woman to meet her in the conference room. Here's how the conversation went:

Manager: "Mary, I need to chat with you about a very delicate topic. It is my hope that you will not be offended but that you will take the feedback and work on what I'm about to share."

Mary: "Of course! What have I done?"

Manager: "You haven't *done* anything. Erm, well, it's just that it's been brought to my attention that you have a very strong body odor. It's my guess that you are probably not even aware because I know you would not want to offend anyone. I would urge you to wash your clothes after each wearing and to give extra attention to your underarm areas when you shower. You may want to consider changing your deodorant. Lastly, you may want to consult a doctor to see if there is something else going on."

Mary: "Thank you so much for letting me know. I really had no idea. I know I perspire a lot, but I didn't know it was offensive to others. I'll pack some wipes and extra deodorant and try to cleanse more often throughout the day. I am so sorry you had to bring this to my attention, and while I'm embarrassed, I'm glad you told me. I really had no idea others were being affected."

The HR leader felt like the weight of the world was off her shoulders. She learned a lot with that experience, and Mary actually started checking with her on occasion to be sure there had been no more complaints.

Hallway Caper

An employee exited an elevator and headed back to her office, but the stench that hit her on the company floor was overwhelming! It seemed someone had an accident outside the elevator door and the droppings lead all the way to the bathroom. It was about 4:00 p.m. on the Friday before Memorial Day, and the office janitorial staff had departed. So, HR was called. HR gets called for everything!

The HR person who received the call was pregnant and could not deal with it. So another employee came to the rescue and treated it as if they were picking up after a dog. She wielded the carpet cleaner, followed by air freshener. Crisis solved. But it left her wondering why the person didn't clean up after him or herself. Was it an employee or some random person? The mystery has never been solved.

Beyond the Call of Duty

This is forever embedded in my brain. The company I had been working for provided me with a brand new Chrysler K car (a smart car, back in the day). As a field insurance claims adjuster, one of my assignments was to go to the train station to pick up a claimant and his wife who were coming into Washington D.C. for a medical evaluation in support of their continuing worker's compensation claim. I had their photo, but I was not given a lot of other information except where to take them for their appointment and what time to return them to the train station. My car was brand new, so no one had ever been in my back seat.

Well, little did I know that the reason I had to pick them up (rather than them renting a car) is that both the husband and wife were mentally challenged. They were a very nice couple, but they really needed an escort. I picked them up and drove them to the doctor's appointment. After the appointment, they were hungry and wanted me to take them to lunch. I found a fast food place. But it was a challenge because the pair had more energy and enthusiasm than I was prepared to deal with.

After lunch, I was heading back to Union Station when I heard the wife say "Uh-oh, I need to go to the bathroom now!" I asked her if she could wait a few minutes, and she said, "I don't think so, I'm bleeding." Her husband was all excited: "She started her period, she started her period! You have to help her!" He was actually jumping up and down in the seat like a little child that was just offered ice cream.

Oh my goodness. I pulled over and looked back—what a mess!

Off we went to the nearest store. I had her tie her sweater

around her waist, and I got her into the bathroom at Kmart where she waited for me to get what she needed, clothes and all. I got them to the train on time, but my afternoon didn't end there. I still had to get rubber gloves and upholstery cleaner to clean my car! I was too embarrassed to take it to a car wash. That was close to twenty-five years ago, and I still remember it like it was yesterday.

Bathroom Confetti

This story comes from a sizable law firm in a major metropolitan city.

One morning, a female entered a bathroom that had several stalls and discovered it looking like Times Square at midnight. All of the toilet paper in the bathroom had been shredded and thrown all around the bathroom. What kind of joke was this? She double checked her calendar: It was not April Fools' Day! This person had been at the firm for quite some time and this had never happened in the past.

For the next few days, this odd phenomenon kept occurring. Each morning, someone would enter the bathroom and found it covered in toilet paper confetti! Who was the culprit and why would they do this? This was a pretty prestigious law practice.

The cleaning company was also getting quite frustrated, and the extra cleaning was costing the firm. This mystery needed to be solved, and quickly. The plan was that the office manager would arrive early and, as each person arrived, she would watch and wait.

The office manager saw one of the female attorneys go in. After a few minutes, she had still not come out. The office manager entered the bathroom and caught the woman as she was shredding and flinging toilet paper! Busted! Needless to say, the attorney was shocked and embarrassed. The office manager was surprised and appalled that an attorney was the culprit.

"What are you doing?" the office manager demanded.

"I'm so sorry—this calms me down," she replied.

As it turned out, this attorney was dealing with medical anxiety, and this behavior was how it manifested itself. Every day, as she drove to the office and thought about her cases, she would get overly anxious and found this therapeutic! Needless to say, the office manager referred her to the employee assistance program and suggested she take some time off.

Footprints

The office manager of this small company received a complaint from a staff member that someone had left their footprints on the wall in a way that makes it appear that their feet are propped on the wall "while doing their business." The office manager was disgusted and frustrated that this would have to be dealt with, after all, this was a professional office—who would do that?

The office manager reacted to the complaint and sent out a scathing email to the staff:

"The fact that I am having to send this email is so very disheartening to me as a manager and as an adult writing to other adults.

Yesterday, I was shown the attached picture—which is footprints on the wall *in the upstairs bathroom. I was later advised that this is not the first time this has happened and, in fact, the footprints have been on the walls and cleaned off numerous times by a different employee who has seen them before.*

The average restroom contains traces of more than 77,000 distinct types of bacteria and viruses, with an average 45% of those being of fecal origin! Why would anyone put their feet on the wall in an office restroom or any room for that matter?

One would assume that it could go without being said, but apparently not, so I will say: Do not place feet on the bathroom wall when in the restroom or any other room of this office. Please keep your feet on the ground.

We've wiped the wall down again and tomorrow our cleaning service will be here to completely disinfect the walls in the restroom.

If you are the person who is the contributor to this wall "art" – STOP!"

Not the best way to handle this as it sounds more like a parent scolding a child, rather than a professional way to deal with this. The company then decided to place the following poster in the bathroom to try to stop this crazy behavior.

FETAL POSITION

A company hosted a large conference. A staff member was to record a very large session and provide small handheld video cameras to the tables to capture some of the group exercises for later use.

The folks who were hosting this session had donated the new cameras because they were also advertising this new product. When it came time to pull out the cameras and use them in the session, it was learned that the staff member in charge of the cameras had not read the directions for the new equipment and had not charged the cameras or purchased batteries as a back-up. She had simply placed the cameras in the box on the tables and expected them to work.

Well, the session leaders were very disappointed because this was a critical part of the session, and they had planned to use the recordings during a follow-on session. When she realized her error, she said nothing, left the room, and was found curled up in a fetal position crying uncontrollably. She was there for about twenty minutes! Nothing anyone said could get her to move on. Such things happen, and no one died. Life goes on!

It was later learned that there had been some personal drama with her boss that contributed to her over-reaction, but in the moment, no one knew how to help her! Needless to say, this is one of those stories that pops up whenever there is a plan to use new equipment at an event: "Did you check

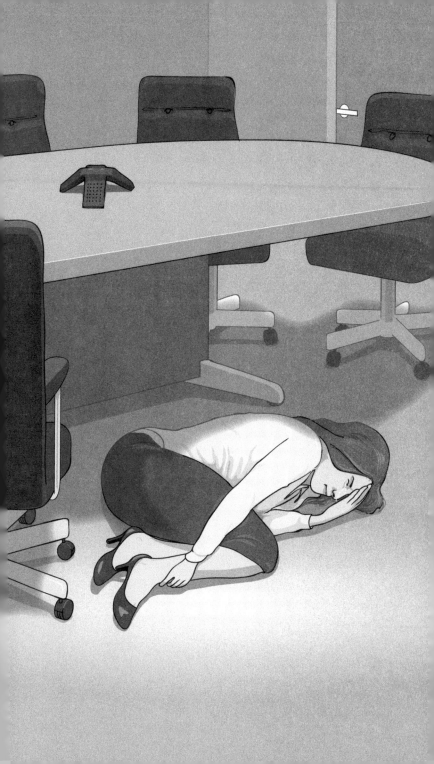

the equipment? Remember what happened at that event when the cameras weren't charged, we don't want anyone going crazy on us again!"

THE BANK OF EMPLOYER

When you earn a mid six-figure income, is it ever appropriate to ask your employer for financial aid? I don't think so, but it happens, according to several folks who provided stories.

One case involved a guy who was very good at his job and made a lot of money (much more than the average person). He came seeking help because he had over-extended himself. He had bought a big house, nice car, fancy vacations, and so on, which put him in a cash-flow crisis because he had bills due that did not coincide with bonus/commission payments. He explained that he was the sole provider for the family, and he didn't want his spouse to know that they were in difficult financial straits! Could he simply get an advance against his "potential" bonus?

There are a few things going on here. The words "potential" and "over-extended" leapt out to the HR person in this case. What if the advance was granted and then the bonus wasn't earned? The employee would find himself in a deeper financial hole. The HR person was also quite concerned about the stress this person was under, given the secretive nature of the request and the stress that poor finances have on individuals. What could creatively be done to help?

The HR person was struck by an idea. The person was looking for a $10,500 advance. He had 250 hours of paid time off sitting on the books and earned $60 an hour. Perhaps the company could cash out 175 hours of time off so as not to increase his debt and clear a few dollars off the finance books? He would have to sign a confidentiality agreement; the company did not want to get into the habit of buying back paid time off because it could get into a bind!

While this one turned out to be a win-win from a dollar perspective, the employee was strongly encouraged to consult with the company employee assistance plan because he definitely needed help with managing his finances within his earnings capacity.

GENDER REASSIGNMENT

While gender changes are becoming more mainstream, this incident happened years ago when the legal protections were in place, but transgender identity was a taboo subject.

An employee had been living a double life—male at work and female after hours. One evening, as a woman, she was in a store in the small town where she lived and saw a coworker enter the store. She was pretty sure that the coworker saw and identified her, but they avoided each other in the aisles.

Evidently, this encounter was wearing on the transgender woman, and a few weeks later she decided to seek some advice, where else but from HR! He (his gender at work) explained to the HR person that he was exploring a gender change. He had been in counseling and was taking the hormone treatments, and he was 90 percent certain he was ready to schedule the surgery. It was his intention that, within the next sixty days, he would be announcing that he would no longer be known as Mark and would be going by Marie from then on. He was looking for support from HR and ensuring HR knew of his legal protections.

The HR person reassured Mark that HR would be with him every step of the way. Mark then let HR know that he feared that he may already be "out" because he was confident that one of the employees recognized him in the store a few weeks prior. Mark wanted HR to check it out with that employee and ensure that he would not be subjected to any tomfoolery about his life choice. HR agreed to check into it.

The following day, the HR person asked to meet with the employee who had seen Mark dressed as a woman. She proceeded cautiously with her questions, and asked him if he had seen Mark in the store a few weeks earlier. The employee stated that he had not seen Mark, but he had seen a female that looked a lot like Mark, smirking as he responded. She then asked if he had told anyone else in the office that he had seen this person. He said, with a chuckle, that he had told his buddies that either Mark had a twin or he had thought it was Halloween, or Mark simply liked to dress as a girl. He said they had a good laugh over it and that was the end of it.

The HR person then proceeded to let him know that he was not to talk about what he had seen with anyone else, and that if anyone were to bring it up, he was not to engage in the conversation. She then proceeded to tell him, with Mark's permission, what Mark's plans were and that it was to be business as usual. Mark is entitled to certain protections under the law, and any conversations, teasing, or whispering would be seen as bullying, and he or others could lose their jobs. This was serious, she told him, and it was her hope that there would be no issues when Mark made it known.

The employee was very gracious and apologetic about his prior behavior. He stated that he really liked Mark, and he felt bad because he knew it must be very hard to go through this. HR could count on him, he said, not to create any issues or drama around this. He went on to state that if Mark wanted to talk with him privately, he would be there for him. WOW!

True to his word, about forty-five days later, on a Friday, Mark let HR know that when he returned to work on Monday, he wanted to be known as Marie and would be dressed as a female. They came up with a plan for an informal memo to come out and let it go. It would be handled as a simple name change, reiterating legal protection language.

Monday came, the memo was in people's inbox when they arrived, and it was a non-event in that workplace. The HR person breathed a huge sigh of relief by close of business on Monday!

Although HR had told Marie that the company would be with her "every step of the way," it was a bit of a misnomer because the company was "self-insured" and so it was not required to cover the cost of the gender reassignment surgery. (Fully insured plans are now required to cover the cost.) If Marie wanted the costs of reassignment surgery covered, she would have to leave the organization and look for a company that was not self-insured in order to get this very expensive process covered. It was a shame to lose such a good employee.

BIZARRE BEHAVIOR

A relatively new female employee started showing some bizarre behaviors that concerned and distracted the team. First, she was aggressively flirting with a contractor who had been working on the team. The contractor kept trying to brush the employee off, until finally he had to get quite insistent to stop her pestering and pursuing a relationship that was not wanted. Soon thereafter, the employee's behavior became very strange.

She started coming into the office stating that she was purchasing and opening a food truck. She had created a Facebook page and had started developing a menu and purchasing food to test out the recipes that she planned to serve. She kept bringing in items, and people were being asked to taste and provide feedback on whether the item should be on the menu or not.

People did not want to eat the samples. The employee would stand next to her colleagues, waiting for them to try the food; it was disruptive and disrespectful! The staff felt quite uncomfortable but didn't want to report the person and create an even more awkward situation with this employee.

Fortunately, as it turned out, this employee needed professional help and no one recognized it before this incident, and she was able to get some treatment. Had someone spoken up earlier, this person could have received help earlier and everyone could have avoided some of the discomfort. It's another see-something-say-something opportunity!

BRING BACK THE MILK!

This was a funny story that occurred when a company was going through some financial challenges.

People were getting laid off, pay raises were being frozen, and a variety of other cost saving measures were being made to keep this company afloat. The facilities leader was tasked with looking at ways to reduce unnecessary spending in the office. This office had, for years, provided a few perks for the employees, among which was having milk delivered to the office. The facilities person decided to cut the milk expense because it was mainly being used for employee's breakfasts, which they brought from home.

One particular employee decided to write to complain directly to the CEO about this expenditure cut and copied in HR. She wrote that it was unacceptable that the office no longer provided milk to have with her cereal in the morning when she arrived at the office. The subject line on the email to the CEO was "Bring Back the Milk!"

The CEO could not believe it. With all that was going on in the office related to cost reductions, why had that employee written to him about such a trivial matter? Did this person not get it? *People are being impacted in many ways—have your cereal at home,* he thought. Here he was dealing with major budget deficits and this person is writing to him about a gallon of milk!

So, the HR person called the employee. They really did

not get it. Apparently, she had enjoyed arriving at the office early to have her breakfast before starting her day. It was convenient to have the milk in the office. The HR person pointed out that there was still a refrigerator there and she should feel free to bring in her own milk. There was really no reasoning with this person, and after a long circular discussion they had to agree to disagree.

You really can't make this shit up!

DOGGY DAY CARE

Not all companies operate like some of the laissez-faire Silicon Valley companies. There are actually lease clauses that govern a lot of things than can and cannot happen in an office building, such as "bring your dog to work."

At one company, there was an employee who started coming in really early. She carried a huge handbag, almost like a beach bag. No one really thought anything about it. She told people that she had a lot of work to do and was coming in early to beat the traffic. That sounded reasonable.

However, on the fourth day of her new work schedule, an employee sitting near her heard a whimper. "What's that sound?" she asked.

"I didn't hear anything," replied the woman.

"You can't hear that whimpering? It sounds like a puppy!"

"Okay, but please don't tell anyone: I have a puppy under my desk. I don't have anyone to watch her while I work."

The colleague was stunned.

Well, it didn't take long for that trust to be broken and the hidden puppy was disclosed. Word is that the puppy was adorable. When she brought it out from under the desk, folks gathered around and there was laughter and cooing in the office. Morale was up and people were happy. But, as you can imagine, someone was allergic, and there was at least one strict rule-follower. Of course, the operations manager who

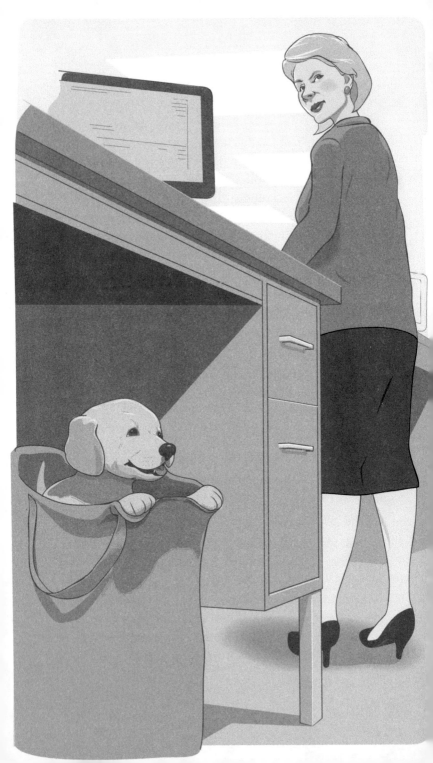

was responsible for the lease was having no part in allowing a puppy in the office!

The puppy owner thought that one of the office administrators "ratted her out," so they had stopped speaking. Although this was not the first time they'd had a tête-à-tête over something in the office, the accused office administrator moved her desk to get away from the hostility. When the HR person who had first heard the puppy learned of the unfolding drama, she took the time to pull the two together to try to make amends. It took a while for them both to cool off, but they eventually started speaking again.

Some wanted the employee reprimanded for breaking a rule, which seemed harsh. It's unfortunate that more companies cannot find ways to bring joy and laughter to an office in such a simple, no cost way. But one good thing to come out of this event was the assembly of a "workplace solutions committee" that was charged with finding ways to solve office disputes before they got out of control and to look for ways to bring the teams together to collaborate and network.

APRIL FOOLS' DAY PRANKS

The president of a carpet-care company loved April Fools' Day antics because they helped morale and made work fun for his team.

For an office mascot, the owner had a "jackalope" created (a cross between a jackrabbit and an antelope). Once the mascot was created, the company had a Facebook contest to name it and the winning name was Dusty. Dusty's strange head was mounted in the reception of the rug-cleaning plant of the company.

Customers who visited the plant would comment on the mascot, and the president would then tell the story of Dusty and show them the other side of it: It seems that he had the back end created as well and installed the doorbell so that when visitors pushed his bottom, the buzzer sounded. This was a year-round joke, not one that was special to April first!

One April Fools' Day, a few of the team came to work early. They took all the chairs and tied them to the ceiling; no small feat for sure. When the workers arrived, they started looking around for their chairs, and the jokers found it hysterical to watch them look everywhere but on the ceiling. This went on for close to an hour and the temperatures started heating up pretty quickly. Some people just can't take a joke!

Birthdays were also sometimes "special" at this company. The president arrived early one day hoping to get some things done before the others arrived. But he was not the first to arrive, and he inquired why another employee was in so early. He was told to go check out a certain person's desk. It had been completely covered in bubble and shrink wrap. That poor employee had to unwrap his desk, and the more he unwrapped, the more frustrated he became, which was incredibly funny for everyone else. Finally, to calm him down, the president assisted him!

The president himself was not immune to the pranks. He arrived one day to find that the wheels to his chair had been removed. He then had to find the wheels that the team had very creatively hidden, using hints they gave him. It was a wheel treasure hunt that took him all over the office and plant. Fortunately, unlike many presidents, this guy loved the camaraderie the joking created in his company. Although, not all of his employees shared his enthusiasm! Perhaps the recruiting team should include some questions about sense of humor to ensure a good cultural fit before actually hiring someone to the team.

FORGOTTEN CAMERA

You just have to love video meetings: You have the opportunity to meet with folks remotely and still be able to see them. It really reduces multitasking and allows for a richer, more engaged experience than using a telephone. But, you do need to remember that you are on video! I am actually the subject of this unfortunate video call event.

I was talking with two of the senior leaders at my company one afternoon. They were seeking my opinion on a few items. The meeting went on, and I was distracted for whatever reason. (I do have a short attention span, especially if I am not really interested in the topic.) I started looking around my desk and focused on a pair of tweezers. I totally forgot that I was on a video call and started tweezing my eyebrows! I am certain that this went on for a few minutes before I suddenly realized ... *CRAP! I'm on video!* Luckily, I had known the two guys I was talking to for at least ten years, and neither one asked, "What the hell are you doing?" Oh, no! They were having way too much fun together laughing at me. None of us acknowledged what had happened at the time.

Several years later, at a leadership meeting, one of the activities was a round-table discussion that included one of the guys from that previous embarrassing call. We were each asked to disclose one of our most embarrassing moments in business. I chose to bring up this story, and the two of us started rolling around laughing about what I had done and the fact that we had never disclosed to each other that we knew about it! It is still fascinating to me that we never talked about it.

Another camera event occurred at a different company. I learned about it later, when someone wanted to hire the subject of this story at our company. It seems that this guy was on a large video call with members of his team, and the manager of this group was leading it. Imagine a *Hollywood Squares* type scenario, where individuals from all over the world could be on the call and the appearances on the monitor look like what you'd see on the TV show. This guy, like everyone else, appeared to be wearing business attire appropriate for the call. But at some point during the call, he stood up to stretch and holy crap! There he was in all of his "glory" in full view of the camera, nothing on from the waist down. Think of the film *The Full Monty* and you'll get the idea. Well, needless to say, that was unforgiveable, and he was now out looking for a job.

Now that story deserves both a "you can't make this shit up" and a "good grief, where's the briefs?"!

HUMAN TAPE MEASURE

One of the biggest challenges when planning a large event is ensuring that the conference and ballrooms will handle the population you are inviting. The leader responsible for the budget and planning usually attends an on-site visit to ensure that the location has represented itself accurately before a contract is nailed down with a venue.

So, on this one occasion, the planning entourage arrives at the venue to meet with the hotel general manager. They are in a large ballroom and the leader asks what size the room is. The general manager isn't sure, and before anyone knows what is happening, the female VP leader says, "I'm six feet tall, so let me figure this out." She lies on the floor and starts doing somersaults all the way down the length of the ballroom, to come up with an estimated size of the room. She had a skirt on and this was in mixed company.

All of the planners just stood there with their mouths open! The venue people were there, her employees were there, and the hired event planning team was there. It all happened so quickly. Finally, someone said, quite dryly, "I'm sure we could have found a tape measure!" They were flabbergasted, but she thought it was funny and efficient.

FLOWER LADY

An employee of this firm appeared to be quite popular and was receiving flowers once, sometimes twice, a week. She would never share the card that came with the flowers and simply stated that a relative or close friend had sent them to her to cheer her up, celebrate an event, or "just because."

One day, the office manager received a call from the florist inquiring about the size of the bill. The firm had used this florist for several years to send flowers for employee birthdays, funerals, birth of a child, and the like. The monthly bill was never especially large for this small firm, but when the office manager asked what the amount was, she learned that it was over $2000! How could that be? As she dug deeper, she learned from the florist that the orders had all been placed by the employee who had been receiving the flowers!

When the office manager confronted the employee she admitted that, yes, she had been using the office account to send herself flowers! She gave no reason, and they had to work out a payment plan to recoup the funds. How in the world could she have thought that she would not be caught?

Once repayment was complete, she no longer worked at that company.

CONFLICT OF INTEREST

At most companies, it is policy that an employee must report any conflict of interest, especially if he or she is the beneficiary of revenue from their employer, whether directly or indirectly. For example, if you have a business in a spouse's name and he or she provides services to your employer, you are required to disclose that information. As a policy, it makes sense, but you read about improprieties all the time, especially in large government contracts.

An employee called a corporate leader and told him that he needed to check out XYZ Company. He told the leader: "I believe it is owned and run by X's spouse. We have been required to use XYZ for the last year, and so I checked out their license. That's all I'm going to say about it, you need to look into it."

So, the leader did. The name on the business license was a generic name, not the employee's name. Unless you looked at the information about the business owner and the address attached to the license, you would not know there was a problem. Even with the last name being different, you would not necessarily suspect impropriety, but the error made by the employee was that the business operated out of his home address.

Before talking with the employee, HR decided to first look at how much had been paid to this company over the past eighteen months. WOW! Over seven figures had been billed by XYZ for services provided to the company! Time to have a real conversation ...

"Hi employee, do you know the name X?"

"Yes, I do," was the reply.

"How do you know X?"

"She owns XYZ Company."

"Are you related to X?"

"Why do you ask that?"

"I ask because we have been told there is a requirement on your team that staff are to use XYZ first before considering another vendor. XYZ has billed us to the tune of seven figures. It's important that we understand the relationship you have with the XYZ owner."

"I use XYZ because they always come through with what we need quickly and they provide an excellent service to our clients."

"Okay, so you still need to answer the question. Exactly how do you know X?"

"What difference does it make?"

"Let me try this another way. Is X your wife?"

"I'm not really happy or comfortable with this line of questioning."

"Well, I'm sorry to hear that, but the question is pretty straightforward and only needs a yes or no response. Are you married to X?"

"Yes."

"Okay, thanks for responding. Did you ever tell anyone at our company that you were married to X prior to suggesting that we use XYZ as a contractor?"

"No, I did not. I do not see the relevance. XYZ gets the job done, and that's what's important."

"So, you don't see the relevance of recommending a company that you benefit from personally when you have your team send work their way? Do you understand conflict of interest?"

"Look, at the end of the day, XYZ Company provides a great solution for our clients, which is all that matters. It's obvious to me from your questions that you are not in agreement, so what happens now?"

"Well, I'll need to chat with legal because your failure to disclose the relationship and the fact that your team sends large quantities of work to XYZ means there is a real conflict of interest. That is against policy and not in keeping with our values."

"You have to be kidding! I'm simply trying to get work done, and you are creating a problem where none exists."

"Well, we'll have to agree to disagree. You are required to disclose these things. We have an ethics policy, and you signed an ethics agreement statement when you were hired. In addition, the reason we are having this conversation is due to the fact that your colleagues are feeling pressure to use XYZ no matter what. They did their own investigation to find out why there is so much pressure to use XYZ, and they brought it to my attention. I'll be in touch shortly."

One probably doesn't need to guess; this person had their last day right after that conversation and he still never understood the problem.

SENATE PRIVILEGE

It had been a long week of meetings and three of us were trying to get home from Boston to Washington, D.C. The flight was oversold and we were trying to get on an earlier flight on standby. One member of our group, when told that there were no seats available innocently asked "what about for a senator?"

The desk agent said, "Oh, Senator So-and-so, we'll do our best to get you on the flight!" Within minutes, he had a seat and was ready to leave myself and our coworker behind! He came back to us and told us the story, and when we asked why he told them he was a senator he replied, "I never said I was a senator, I simply asked if the flight was sold out even for senators!" We all had a great laugh as the desk agent never asked him if he was a senator and never asked him to show credentials. They simply assumed from his question that he must be a senator! We teased him that if we didn't get on the flight we were going to turn him in (of course we wouldn't do that, but it was fun to tease him!).

At the end of the day, we all made the earlier flight and still laugh about this many years later.

EPILOGUE

This has been a fun book to write. It spans many years of business leadership and human resources leadership. I have enjoyed a fantastic career, and while I truly loved being a business leader, my time in human resources brought me the greatest satisfaction.

Much has changed in HR over the years. Just in terms of jargon, we have seen a change from "personnel," to "human resources," and now "people and culture." Within the field of HR, the ways in which the functions of various HR professionals are described have changed, too; for example, someone who once worked in "recruiting" now works in "talent attraction," and those responsible for "training" are now responsible for "learning and development," and a "generalist" is now a "business partner," and so it goes.

These days, the line between personal time and professional time has almost disappeared, and social media has brought a myriad of new challenges for leaders, legal advisors, and HR. The openness with which people share information about their lifestyle, workplace (including specific colleagues), beliefs, and politics would have been inconceivable just a decade ago. People use poor or disrespectful language, share "out there" opinions, and post images they really shouldn't. At the same time, however, people seem more sensitive about everything and are less tolerant when a sincere mistake has been made, and the daily news shows like to report disrespectful behavior. People no longer listen in order to understand or empathize; they appear to be listening to disagree or challenge opinions.

As I write this epilogue, the news is saturated with people disclosing mistreatment, disrespectful, illegal behaviors from all industries, businesses, and government agencies. The #METOO movement has taken off. I was recently asked what is the most challenging thing that leaders will face going forward; in my opinion, it's finding the right talent with good cultural fit; keeping up with rapid change to remain relevant; and navigating through the alleged hostile work environment behaviors that are surfacing. The personal and business impact is huge. The cost to the organization for legal expenses, protecting the brand image, and safeguarding the overall internal culture will consume many hours of a leader's time and many dollars to the business, whether it's to educate or to investigate or to defend.

All these changes mean that the world of HR is going to continue to be both a challenging and rewarding environment to work in. And now, more than ever, HR is a strategic business partner and not an administrative arm of a company. The number-one role for people in HR is to protect the corporate assets. That is done by strategic programs and education to ensure that companies create an inclusive, diverse workforce that accepts, listens, and encourages engagement and collaboration among all employees. Creating a great place to work is the responsibility of everyone in the organization, but it must be led by a strong, professional HR team supported by the senior leadership team.

I miss getting the daily calls from around the world by people who say, "Denise, I have a story for your book ..."

Perhaps there will be a sequel as I gather more stories! But I will always enjoy being involved in the field of leadership and professional coaching, helping to change behaviors and to make the world a better place to live and work.

I encourage you to bring your best self to your place of employment and good things will come your way.

Best, Denise

ABOUT THE AUTHOR

An award-winning visionary leadership coach, HR executive, speaker, and educator with a passion for people, Denise founded Thallo Leadership Consulting, an executive coaching and leadership development firm. She is the former SVP of HR for a global IT company. Denise serves on the Citizens Review Board for Children in Maryland and is a member of the Leadership Master Mind Alliance in Orlando, Florida.

Denise holds a Bachelor of Science degree in Technical Management from the University of Maryland University College and a Master of Science degree in Applied Behavioral Science from Johns Hopkins University. Denise is a Certified Professional Coach and a certified Senior Professional in Human Resources with HRCI, as well as a SHRM Senior Certified Professional. She was recognized as a Top 100 Women of the Channel in *CRN* magazine in 2010.

Denise is married to her high school sweetheart, Tony, and they have two children and seven grandchildren. Denise makes her home in Annapolis, Maryland, and Rehoboth Beach, Delaware.